Henry The Sixth, The First Part

by John Crown

1681

A FACSIMILE PUBLISHED BY CORNMARKET PRESS
FROM THE COPY IN THE BIRMINGHAM SHAKESPEARE LIBRARY
LONDON
1969

PUBLISHED BY CORNMARKET PRESS LIMITED
42/43 CONDUIT STREET LONDON W1R ONL
PRINTED IN ENGLAND BY FLETCHER AND SON LIMITED NORWICH

SBN 7191 0133 6

HENRY the Sixth,

The First PART.

WITH THE

MURDER

OF HUMPHREY

Duke of Glocester.

As it was Acted at the

Dukes Theatre.

Written by Mr. *CROWN*.

LONDON,

Printed for *R. Bentley*, and *M. Magnes*, in *Ruſſel-Street*, in *Covent-Garden.* 1681.

PR
2878
.K3
C7
1969

The Prologue.

WIth much ado a Prologue we obtain'd,
    From th' Author who this good old Play did mend,
    He said a Prologue was a Painted Clout,
Only to tell the Shew within, hung out,
And he no pains wou'd on the Clout bestow,
When very few wou'd come to see the Show.
The Comet that last Summer flam'd obove,
Has dropt his Pitch in every Dish you love.
Poor slighted Wit is flung among the Swine,
Like Grapes in France, now you forbid their Wine.
Play-Houses like forsaken Barns are grown,
The lusty Threshers of both ends of Town.
Let the Corn rot, and give their Labour o're,
And so the Vizards cackle here no more:
Or if they hither come 'tis but for fear,
Lest zealous Constables find 'em elsewhere,
And their torn Coats for Romish Reliques seize,
And the poor Girles for Painted Images.
Thus all your Pleasures wither and decay,
You 've suck'd the Globe, and flung the shell away.
As for our wretched selves we are forc'd still,
To chaw down Poetry against our will,
But little Pleasure it to us does give,
We swallow it as Sick-Men eat, to live.
And to preserve your Stomacks we make bold,
To Cram you every day with New or Old.
To day we bring old gather'd Herbs, 'tis true,
But such as in sweet Shakespears Garden grew.
And all his Plants immortal you esteem,
Your Mouthes are never out of taste with him.
Howe're to make your Appetites more keen,
Not only oyly Words are sprinkled in;
But what to please you gives us better hope,
A little Vineger against the Pope.

The Persons Represented in the PLAY.

King *Henry* the Sixth,   By Mr. *Jos. Williams.*

Humphry Duke of *Glocester*, Lord Protector of the Kingdom, and Uncle to the King, being Brother to King *Henry* the 5th,   By Mr. *Batterton.*

The *Cardinal* ——— a Bastard Son of *John* of *Gaunt*, and so Uncle to Duke *Humphry*.   By Mr. *Harris.*

Richard Plantagenet, Heir of the House of *York*, pretender to the Crown.   By Mr. *D. Williams.*

Duke of *Buckingham*.

Earl of *Warwick*.

Earl of *Salisbury*.

Duke of *Suffolk*, a Lover of the Queen.   By Mr. *Smith.*

Queen *Margaret*, Wife of King *Henry* the 6th, in Love with the Duke of *Suffolk*.   By my La. *Slingsby.*

Elianor, Duchess of *Glocester*, Wife to the Lord Protector.   By Mrs. *Batterton.*

Sheriff of *London*, Sir *John Stanly*.   *Attendants.*

SCENE, The Court at *Westminster.*

TO

TO
Sir CHARLES SIDLEY
BARONET.

SIR,

I Am afraid I shall displease you, by setting your Name, before so scandalous a thing as a Pamphlet of mine; but when I have told you the reason, I believe you will pardon me. I make not use of your Name to add a lustre to mine; I am not so much concerned for it. Fame built on Poetry is like a Castle in the Air, which the next Wind demolishes. I have heard of great Armies Mustered in the Air, but never of any thing they Conquered. Such are the Forces of Poetry, I have had my Ears torn with the noise of a Poets Drums and Trumpets, of the Bellowing of his Actors, and the clapping of his Audience, but I never heard of one inch of firm Land he gained. All he fought for was Inchanted Ground, which now he seems to possess, and anon it vanishes, has nothing real in it but the vexation of obscene Birds, which disturb him with their croaking, whilst he wakes, and defile him by muting upon him if ever he sleeps. No wise Man can much regard what his share is in such a barren and floating Place.

My concernment is for some little Truth and good Sense, Commodities which no one will expect to find aboard such a Paper Boat, as a Play, were it not convoy'd by so flourishing and great Reputation as yours. I speak not my own, but the opinion of some of the wisest Men of this Age, this Play is no indifferent Satyre upon the most pompous fortunate and potent Folly, that ever reigned over the minds of men, called Popery. My Lord Bacon says, good Books ought to have no other Patrons but Truth and Reason. Many other things ought to be, that never will. If Truth and Reason were things so potent, how came Folly and Error to prevail over e'm in all Ages and Nations? How came Wisdom to live among the Antients in Porches and Tubs, and Fools to shine in Palaces whilst living, and in Temples when dead? How came Truth among Christians to be troden under foot, for several hundreds of Years, whilst Error and Folly rode on mens Shoulders, and trod on Princes Necks? Mens Shoulders had never been so ill us'd, if their Heads had been good. And when a Germane Fryar discovered Truth, by an accident as strange as another did

Gun

The Epistle Dedicatory.

Gunpowder, how came the latter mischievous invention, to have fifty times the success of the former, and to pierce a hundred times as many Heads and Hearts? If Truth in Schools and Churches meet so much contempt, what must it expect in so wretched a thing as a Play is now esteemed? The wisest Men among the Ancients indeed, thought themselves scarce wise enough to judge Drammatique Poetry, but ours think themselves much too Wise, and throw it off as a Trifle for Women and Fools to play with; and by that means it pines more and more into a Trifle. For what vigour soever is necessary to please Ladies elsewhere, Impotence best delights e'm upon the Stage. The Poets that will hit the right Mark, must aim at the Boxes, and what Arrows they shoot over them are all lost, nor are our Male Judges of a more Masculine Spirit. I have always observed when an Actor talks Sense, the Audience begins to sleep, but when an unnatural passion sets him a grimacing and howling as if he were in a fit of the Stone, they immediately waken, listen, and stare, as if some rare Operator were about to Cut him: In short, Sense is so great a stranger to the most, that it is never welcome to Company for its own sake, but the sake of the Introducer. For this reason I use your Name to guide that share of it is in this Play through the Press, as I did Shakespear's to support it on the Stage. I called it in the Prologue Shakespear's Play, though he has no Title to the 40th part of it. The Text I took out of his Second Part of Henry the Sixth, but as most Texts are serv'd, I left it as soon as I could. For though Shakespear be generally very delightful, he is not so always. His Volumn is all up-hill and down; Paradise was never more pleasant than some parts of it, nor Ireland and Greenland colder, and more uninhabitable then others. And I have undertaken to cultivate one of the most barren Places in it. The Trees are all Shrubs, and the Men Pigmies, nothing has any Spirit, or shape; the Cardinal is duller then ever Priest was. And he has hudled up the Murder of Duke Humphry, as if he had been guilty of himself, and was afraid to shew how it was done: But I have been more bold, to the great displeasure of some, who are it seems ashamed of their own mysteries, for there is not a Tool us'd in the murder of Duke Humphry in this Play, but what is taken out of their own Church Armory, nor a word put into the mouth of the Cardinal and his foolish Instruments, but what first dropt from the Heads that adorn their own Church Battlements. I cou'd be large in Quotations did I not nauseate Pedantry. I shall only shew that what serves here to make the Comical part of a Play, does in the Popish Countries compose the gravest part of their Devotion. I make the foolish Murderer complain that he cou'd not thrive, though he kept every Day a Holy-day in honour of some Saint. Now nothing is more known then that in those Countries, the great Trafique between them and their Saints, almost ruine all other Trades. The People are forced to keep so many Holy-days, that they have not Working-days enough to keep themselves; when they shou'd be labouring to fill their Bellies, they are cramming Latine into their Mouths, in the honour of some Saint, who perhaps understands not a word of the Language, unless he learnt it since he died, which is a great doubt. And they have so many Saints, that the People in Heaven starve those upon Earth, and contrary to what is done in other Famines, the Dead devour the Living. No Manufactury

The Epistle Dedicatory.

dustry thrives like that of Saint-making, all others must contribute to that, and even the Workmanship of God must grow poor to enrich that of the Priests. When all the Saints had disappointed this poor Fellow, I make him go to a Priest for advice, who instead of bidding him follow his calling, sets him a mumbling a Prayer, which he tells him is of that efficacy, that if he says it over Thirty Days together, it will procure him in the end what ever he asks for. What appears too ridiculous here for the mouth of a Stage-fool, in a Country no less polished then France, is recommended to the Faith and Devotion of no less a Prince then the Dauphin, in a little Book entitnled,

> HEVRES Dedidees a Monsiegneur le Dauphin, contenant L' Office qui se dit en L' Eglise, avec l' Exercice du Matin, & en soir, & le Catechisme dresse par les Peres de la Mission.

The Prayer is to the Virgin Mary, in the 229th Page, in the middle of the Prayer 'tis said, —— *Here demand what ever you please.*

When this Prayer would not do, I make the Priest give him another, conveyed by an Angel as he says into the Grave of a Germane Lady, who had her Head cut off, and lived after it two and twenty Hours, not being able to die, till she had Confessed and Communicated. And the Prayer had this miraculous power annext to it, that whosoever did but carry it about him, shou'd never suffer by Sea or by Land, &c. This I found in a little French Book of Devotion to the Virgin Mary, Licenced by the Fathers of the Augustine Friars, as containing nothing in it contrary to Catholick Faith, and recommended to the People with an extraordinary Approbation; by what Charter these Prayers claim such great Priviledges, is not said, yet must be believed. Some think me very profane, for bringing what belongs to the Church upon the Stage; but they may allow me that, since they have carried many things that belong to the Stage into the Church. To expose these Follies to the People is the business of this Play, and I believe you will pardon me that I borrow some assistance from your Reputation, since you your self have of late to your very great Honour, employ'd your Interest and excellent Understanding in the same design. And though you can do it better in common Conversation, then I by all my Study and Premeditation, It follows not, because Lightning sometimes shoots through all the Heavens, and rends the Oaks, a Man may not light a Candle in the Night: To hinder this Rush light from being blown out, is the reason why I place your Name before it. I have a mind the Play shou'd be read, and every one will read it, if they think you like it. I know few Understandings so universally esteem'd as yours, and for so good Reason. It wou'd be foolish in me to lash out into unnecessary praises of a Wit that has been so long the delight and ornament of the Nation, and is now become the Defence of what is very dear to it, Truth, Liberty, and Property. I have so deeply felt, what the loss of Property is, that I cannot but honour the Defenders of it, though their defence comes too late to me. I may appear vain in my complaint, but People will Groan when they are in pain; my Father, and by consequence my self, his Heir, was stript long since (by the advice of some ill great Men, who sacrifice

both

The Epistle Dedicatory.

both private and publick Interest to their own) of the Moity of a Province so considerable, the French Crown thought it worth contending for, many Years. And if that fortunate Kingdom strove for it, you may imagine they got it. I have great hopes of a speedy reparation from the great Justice Clemency and Goodness of his Majesty. But this loss made me run into that Madness, call'd Poetry, and inhabit that Bedlam, call'd a Stage. I have been so happy, that for several Years, certain Gentlemen unknown to me, have fallen on me, and endeavoured to Bleed me when ever I appear'd. I wish I knew 'em, that I might thank 'em for the Kindness they have done me, though they design'd me nothing but Mischief. The grounds of their Antipathy I know not. Fools I confess may be very well moved to bark at Poets, from the same cause, that they say all kind of Dogs do at Skinners, from a natural instinct that gives 'em notice their own Hides are in danger. But I have no great scent of Blood upon me, and therefore must impute their Aversions to those Occult Qualities that puzle Philosophers. This convinces me, 'tis necessary for me to flie to some Wise Mans protection; and I cannot be safer than under yours. Poets are too poor to be beg'd, 'tis well if they can get Guardians for begging. I am confident you will be entreated to take upon you the Guardianship of this little parcel of a Mad-mans Estate, now I have told you for what good uses it 'tis design'd. And if so, this will do well, and I shall live at ease, for those who will behave themselves very rudely to me as a Poet, and to this as a thing for publick entertainment, will be very civil to this when it is under your care, and to me when I am received by you: For

SIR,

Your very humble Servant,

JOHN CROWN.

Henry

Henry the Sixth;

OR, THE

MURDER

OF THE

Duke of Glocester.

The First Part.

ACT. I.

Enter Humphry *Duke of* Glocester, *Duke of* York, *Cardinal* Beauford, *Duke of* Somerset, *Duke of* Buckingham, *Earl of* Salisbury, *Earl of* Warwick.

Glo. MY Lords, you cannot but have seen of late
Much discontent sit always on my Brow.
All Men that know me well, must know, no private
Petty concernment can unfix my mind.
No; (some will think perhaps I speak too proudly,
I care not what they think, I'le speak my Mind)
Nothing has weight enough to press my spirits
Less than the great Misfortunes of the Kingdom.

Card. So! how my Lord Protector gracefully ——— *aside.*
Ushers himself into these Lords esteem?
What bosom here now will not bid him wellcome?
I hate him, but I will not let him know it,
Till I can let him know it to his ruine.

Glo. Ah!

Glo. Ah! my Lords, Did my valiant glorious Brother,
Henry the Fifth, erect the Law of *England*
Above the *Roman,* or the *Macedonian?*
Do things, that made the Continent all tremble,
When e're the favourable Winds unlockt
The floating Gates of this our little World,
To let out that our brave Warriors to invade it,
That *France* not only did confess it self
A Vassal to his Royal *English* Blood;
But the whole Empire of the World did seem
To own it self the Birth right of his Valour?

Yo. Eternity shall ne'r wear out the Characters
Of his Renown, which his keen Sword engrav'd.

Glo. Ay, yes his fame shall last; but not his Empire:
He's dead, and with him his great Empire dies:
All that his Valour got, all that the vigilance
And wisdom of my Brother *Bedford* kept:
All that your selves and I, have early and late
Study'd to keep, and kept some years with glory,
Crowning our King in *Paris* in his Infancy,
Making Proud *France* bow to an *English* Child.
All, all these Labours, Victories and Glories,
Are melting down in a soft beautious bosom,
Given away to purchase a Fair Face.
A fatal Marriage in one fatal minute
Has spoyl'd the Work of many glorious years.

Card. Nephew, you are more passionate than needs;
France is not gone, nor shall it go so easily.

Glo. No, 'tis not gone indeed, but all the sluces
Are pulling up, and it is going fast.
'Tis pouring out apace in Provinces;
The new made Duke of *Suffolk* gives whole Provinces
To buy the King a Wife, *Anjou* and *Maine*
Are frankly given to the Queen's poor Father
King *Reignier,* whose high and flowing style
Dwells far above the Banks of his low Purse,
But he must have these Provinces to fill it.
Of such low value, in this Duke's esteem,
Is all the purchase of our Blood, that he
Wil give it all away for Blushing Cheeks.

Sal. Those Dukedoms were the Keys of *Normandy.*
My Lord of *Warwick* Weeps———Why weeps my Son?

War. Who wou'd not weep to see his own Blood cheapned
And sold before his Face at a low rate?
I won those Provinces, and what I got
With Wounds, is given away with peaceful words.

Glo. Yes,

The MURDER of the D. of GLOCESTER.

Glo. Yes, and to make it even ridiculous,
The Duke of *Suffolk* Asks a whole Fifteenth
For Charges, to Transport the Queen to *England*.
What? Was there ne'r a Beauty in the World
Besides the Queen? yes, sure there was in *England*;
Had the King so much doted upon Beauty,
He might have Married one of His fair Subjects,
And had more Beauty at a cheaper rate.

Card. My Lord of *Glocester*, this is hot discourse,
And, as I think, to very little purpose;
Since what is done, now cannot be recall'd;
And what is done, was done to please the King.

Glo. My Lord of *Winchester* I understand you;
'Tis not my hot Discourse, but Presence warms you.
You have a Fester'd Mind, and 'twill break out;
I saw it in your Face; if I stay longer
We shall begin our antient Bickerings:
But such small matters shall not trouble me,
I will be gone; but e're I go I'le Prophesy,
France will be lost: but I desire to prove
As False a Prophet, as you are a Priest ―――*Exeunt.*

Card. Affronted thus? 'Pox o' these fumbling Robes! *(aside.)*
How came my Warlike Spirit wrapt in these
Formalities, that hold my hands from Blood?
I'm fitter for a Sword, and I will use one―――
Did you not hear the good Protector, Lords?
Expect what usage you will have; when I
His Unckle, and a Priest, am thus abus'd.
You see how well his Enmity is heal'd;
And he has much the same kindness for you,
And indeed for the King. He makes great shew
Of Zeal for *England*, and he has great zeal for it
That is t'enjoy it; he is heir apparent;
And the King cannot please him by a Marriage,
Unless he'd Wed an Altar, or a Cell.
Be not, my Lords, cheated with his smooth words.
What though the foolish common people dote on him,
Clapping their hands, and shouting when they see him,
Crying, Heaven save your Royal Excellence,
And call him always the good Duke of *Glocester*?
They are Fools, and know not Men, nor what they love;
Uncheat e'm; but however save the King,
Protect him from his dangerous Protector.

Buck. Why shou'd the King, my Lords, have a Protector?
He is of age (I think) to rule himself.
My Lord of *Somerset* joyn you with me,

B 2

We

HENRY the SIXTH; or,

We, with the Duke of *Suffolks* ayd, will hoyse
Duke *Humphry* from his Seat.
   Card. This weighty business
Brooks no delay; I'le to the Duke of *Suffolk*———*Exit.*
   Som. Though the Protector's Pride and Greatness vex us,
The Cardinal's Insolence is more intolerable;
If *Gloster* be displac'd he'l be Protector.
   Buck. If *Gloster* falls, or you or I'le succeed——— *Ex.* Buck. *and* Sal.
   Sal. So! so! the Kingdom will thrive well no doubt,
When all will rend her for their private ends.
I never saw but the good Duke of *Glocester*
Bore himself like a Noble Gentleman;
But I have seen the Cardinal demean himself
More like a Soldier than a Priest; he'l often
Swear like a Ruffian, quarrel like a Hector,
Trample on all, as he were Lord of all:
My worthy Son, and you my Lord of *York*,
My valiant Brother, let us joyn together,
And shew the Kingdom has some good Men in it,
Who faithfully will serve their King and Country,
And ayd all others who promote that work,
And among those I reckon the Protector.
   War. So heaven help me, as I love my Country.—(*Ex.* Sal, *&* War.
   Yo. And so say I, for I have greatest cause,
Anjou and *Main* are given to the *French*.
Two Dukedoms given for a Dukes fair Daughter.
Henry, I blame thee not: What is it to thee?
Thou dost not give away thine own, but mine.
Pirates may make cheap penny-worths of their Pillage.
Whilst the poor injur'd owner stands aloofe,
And shakes his head, and weeps, and wrings his hands,
And sees his Goods all borne away, and dares
Not touch his own, or scarcely call it his.
England, and *France*, and *Ireland*, are my Kingdoms,
One day I may both claim and seize my own,
And from weak *Henry*'s Head may pull the Crown:
These high fierce Tempests methinks make it shake.
What opportunity they give, I'le take.   (*Exit.*

   Enter Duke of Glocester, *and his Dutchess* Elianor.

   Eli. Why droops my Lord, and on the sullen Earth
Fixes his Eyes? What dost thou there behold
King *Henry*'s Diadem fallen from his Head,
Too feeble to support the mighty weight?
If it be that thou look'st on, gaze thy fill,

The MURDER of the D. of GLOCESTER.

Put forth thy hand, and reach the glorious Gold.
   Glo. Oh *Nell!* sweet *Nell!* if thou dost love thy self,
Banish the Canker of Ambitious thoughts,
They will devour thy Peace, thy Life, thy Soul.
May the curst hour, when I imagine ill
Against my Royal Nephew, vertuous *Henry,*
Be my last breathing in this mortal World.
   Eli. I wish the same to me ; but, Is it ill
To the good Pious King, to take from him
A heavy Weight that presses him to Earth,
An Element his heavenly mind abhors ?
His thoughts are all above, and Royal cares
Tear e'm, and pull e'm down to earth in spite of him,
And, What a torment to him must that be ?
It is unjust to let so good a Prince
So cruelly be tortur'd with a Crown.
   Gloc. Oh *Elianour!* away with thy fond words,
Thou mayst deceive thy self, thou canst not me:
Hast thou in my Embraces layn so long,
And am I yet wholly a stranger to thee ?
I find thy high aspiring thoughts did study
My honor, and my offices, not me.
Thou know'st them well, thou hast weigh'd them exactly,
But me thou art an utter stranger to,
Or thou woud'st never tempt me to disloyalty.
   Eli. He is the loyal Subject seeks to please
His King, and not himself: 'Tis more disloyalty
T'impose a Crown upon Religious *Henry,*
Than 'tis to Usurp one from another King.
But you are only Loyal to your self,
And your own fame ; because to take the Crown
The World wou'd call Disloyalty and Treason ;
You wrong the King, to save your own renown.
   Glo. Away, away fond *Elianor!* ——— as Nature
Has given you Women thinner skins than Men,
Through which your working blood is easier seen ;
So thinner Arts to hide your laboring thoughts.
Do not I know your thoughts, designs, and soul,
And all you'd work me to as well as you ?
You would have me throw my self down to Villany,
To exalt you in place above the Queen.
Blast my Renown and Soul to all eternity,
To please your haughtiness for some few years.
Oh *Elianor?* now I must Chide outright ;
Presumptuous, unkind, ill-minded *Elianor!*
Are you not the second Woman in the Kingdom ?

                                                        Have

Have you not Worldly Pleasure at command?
A greater circle of delight, than all
Thy Soul can range about in thy whole Life?
Yet not content with these, Wilt thou be forging
New impious honors, till pil'd heap on heap
They fall, and overwhelm thy self and me?

   Eli. I must confess I mortally abhor,
And scorn that Woman, which is now my Queen
Oh! hateful thought! she! she! my Queen —— a Vassal
Of *France* subdu'd by us into a Province;
And she a Beggar in that Conquer'd Province,
Become the Queen, and Mistriss of her Conquerors;
I the first Woman of Victorious *England*,
Bow to the last of low dejected *France?*
Preposterous! ignominious! base! contemptible!
Had you the spirit of an English Conqueror,
You wou'd not bear it——but you have it not.
The mighty fire, that burnt so bright and hot
In the brave English Souls of the last Age,
Is blazing now its last in me a Woman;
Who can no more than greatly think and talk;
A shrewd sign heaven is taking from us *France,*
Since he takes from us spirits that shou'd rule it.
And yet were I but Queen of *England* once,
I wou'd not doubt but to keep Conquer'd *France.*
Though Kings, and Lord Protectors cannot do it.

   Glo. Talk not of ruling Kingdoms, rule your self.
That I lament the King's most fatal Marriage,
The Queen her self, and all the Kingdom knows:
But I abhor it not for Womanish causes,
Because my Wive's inferior goes before her;
But because *France*, *England's* inferior,
Will by this Match ascend above her Conqueror:
We give two Provinces to buy a Wife,
Who brings nought with her but a shameful Peace,
And this is that causes my present sadness.

   Eli. And sadness will redress your Country's Griefs.

   Gl. Yes! He shall dye that wrought e'm, trayterous *Suffolk.*

   Eli. If *Suffolk* dyes for bringing such a Curse on us,
What shou'd be done to her who is that Curse?
Let her not live, or rather let her live,
But live no Queen ——

   Glo. But subject to your self ——

   Eli. I almost scorn to have so poor a Subject.

   Glo. Ah, *Elianor!* thy Pride, and my fond Love
To thee, will bring destruction on us both.

The MURDER of the D. of GLOCESTER.

Have I not Griefs enow already on me,
And Enemies enow that plot my ruine?
But you must be among the number of e'm?
   Eli. I'em Enemy to nothing but the Queen;
And I'le to her be an implacable
And Devillish Enemy, whil'st she is a Queen:
Let her be poor Dame *Margaret*, and my Subject,
And I will Sign her then an Act of Grace.
   Glo. You will comply in nothing to please me.
   Eli. I will comply in every thing I can;
But I must hate the Queen in spite of me.
   Glo. If thou must hate her, do; but yet love me.
   Eli. I hope you doubt not that, my Lord.
   Glo. I do not.

Enter a Messenger.

   Messen. My Lord Protector, 'tis His Majesties pleasure
You prepare to ride to S*.* *Albans*,
Where both the King and Queen are a going to Hawke.
   Glo. I go! —— Come *Nell*—— Wilt thou along with us? —— *Ex.*
   Eli. Yes, my good Lord, I'le follow presently.
Follow —— I that's the Word —— follow I must,
Whil'st *Glocester* bears this base and humble mind.
My Spirit cries, go first; the Duke sayes, follow:
Shall I obey my Husband, or my Soul?
My Soul is my self, he but my other self;
And by his humble mind my weaker self:
Well, I will play my part in Fortune; Pageant
Where are you there? Sir *John* —— nay, fear not Man,
We are alone, here's none but thee and I.

Enter Humes.

   Hume. Heaven preserve your Majesty.
   Eli. My Majesty?
   Hume. Yes, that will be your Title very shortly.
   Eli. Has my infernal friend the Devil said this,
By his Priest and Priestess the Conjurer and Witch?
Hast thou conferr'd with e'm?
   Hume. Madam I have.
   Eli. And Will they undertake to do me service?
   Hume. They have promised from the infernal deeps to dragge
One of the Spirits that of old gave Oracles,
Whose fiery eye, by its own Native Light,
Sees all that's hidden in Fates dark Abyss,

HENRY the SIXTH; or,

As plain as we Mortals when they come to light:
This Spirit shall make Answer to all Questions,
That it shall please your Grace to pose him with.

   Eli. It is enough. I'le think upon the Questions.
Here, *Hume*, take this reward, make merry Man
With thy Confederates in this weighty business.

   Hume. I humbly thank your Grace ———   *Exit.*

Enter the Duke of Suffolk *talking with the* Queen.

   Eli. See, here comes she
That blasts my eyes worse than the Spirit can do
The Witch will raise out of th' Infernal deep;
And with her, her damn'd Minion, Trayterous *Suffolk*.
That I were now a Pestilence to cover her
From head to foot with tort'ring deadly sores.
I will throw scorn on her as I pass by,
A thing a Woman hates worse than the Plague.
And I will undermine her Royal Glories,
If digging deep as lowest Hell will do it.
I'le climbe the Throne, or else to Hell I'le fall;
If Heaven won't make me great, the Devil shall.

   Qu. Ha! Did you not observe, my Lord of *Suffolk*,
With what contempt that Woman look'd upon me,
As she past by?

   Suff. I saw it, and I laugh'd at it.

   Qu. Ho! call her back, and fling her at my feet.

   Suff. She shall fall shortly there, and lower too,
If my Plots fail not.———

Enter Petitioners, Peter *the Armorers Man being one.*

   1. *Pet.* May it please your Grace.

   Suff. What woud'st thou have with me?

   1. *Pet.* I think you be my Lord Protectors Grace,
If you be, pray your Grace see my Petition.

   2. *Pet.* And mine.

   3 *Pet.* And mine.———an't please your Grace,

   Qu. So, All Petitions to the Protector's Grace,
The Kingdom's supplications all to him,
And all the Ladies follow his Wives Train:
The King and I are only Royal Cyphers,
Flourish'd and guilded only with fine Titles.
Come, What are your Petitions? let me see e'm.

   1. *Pet.* Mine is, an't please you Madam, against *John Goodman*, my
Lord Cardinall's Man, for keeping my House, and my Lands, and my
Wife from me.

                                                           Suff. How?

The MURDER of the D. of GLOCESTER.

Suff. How? thy Wife from thee too? that's very hard.

1. *Pet.* Nay, an't please your Grace, let him give me my House and my Lands, and let him keep my Wife an' he will, I do not care, now he has had her so long.

Suff. What's yours? What's here? Against the Duke of *Suffolk*, for Enclosing the Commons of *Melford*? How now you Rascal?

2. *Pet.* An't please your Grace I am but a poor Petitioner of our whole Township.

Pet. Mine is against my Master *Thomas Horner*, for saying, the Duke of *York* is lawful Heir to the Crown.

Qu. How?

Pet. Yes, and that the King is but an Usurper.

Qu. There's a Villain indeed.

Suff. Who is there?

Enter a Servant.

Take this Fellow in, and send for a Pursuivant presently,
We'l hear more of this Matter before the King.

Qu. You, here; who shroud your selves under the Protector,
Begin your Suits anew, and sue to him.   (*Tears their Petitions.*
This is the Duke of *Suffolk*, I'me your Queen.

2 *Pet.* The Duke of *Suffolk*! oh! I am undone!

Qu. Away you Slaves! ho! turn these Fellows out.
Is this the Fashion in the Court of *England*?
Is this the Royalty of th' English King,
To be a Pupil to a Governour?
Am I a Queen, yet Subject to a Duke?
Oh my *La Poole*! when in the City *Tours*
Thou rann'st a tilt in honour of my Love,
And stol'st away the Ladies hearts of *France*;
I from thy Graces copyed in my Mind
A charming glorious Picture of King *Henry*;
I thought thy Courage, Courtship, and Proportion,
Had been brave Shadows, of thy braver King.
But oh! there ne'r was Woman so deceiv'd
At the first sight of the Kings sad grave Look;
The golden Image of him in my mind
Fell down upon my heart, and almost broke it.
My heavy heart sunk in a Royal shadow,
And greater was the fall, because before
It stood on high and golden expectations.
Ah! never was so sad a fall, as that
From glorious *Suffolk*, down to soft King *Henry*.

Suff. Madam, be patient, for I Married you,
Not to the poor weak King, but to the brave Kingdom,

C   And

And that I'le make a glorious Husband to you.

Qu. Indeed the Marriage 'tween the King and me
Is but a strange one; for to speak the truth,
I'm Wedded to the Throne more than to him,
And he is Married more to Heaven than me.
His Soul is Married to all the Saints in Heaven;
Heaven is the King's spacious Seraglio:
There his heart lives; that which he leaves below
With me, and with the Kingdom, is a shadow.

Suff. He is indeed no more but a King's Ghost,
That walks in night; it has been night in *England*
E'r since that Glorious Sun, his Father, set.
And *France* and *England*, like two metled Steeds
Bound, startle, break their reins, and run away,
At sight of this pale Ghost; nor will be Govern'd.

Qu. 'Twere night with *England*, I am sure with me,
If 'twere not for my glorious *La Poole*.
If 'twere not for thee, *England*, were Hell to me,
And I tormented with Infernal pains,
Under the Arrogance of the Protector,
Of Cardinal *Beauford*, that imperious Church-Man,
Of *Somerset*, *Buckingham*, and grumbling *York*,
For each of these is greater than the King.

Suff. And *Salisbury*, and *Warwick* are as great as they.

Qu. Indeed, for any thing that I can see,
The King's the only Subject in the Kingdom.
He obeys all, and no one obeys him.
But all this does not vex me half so much,
As the intolerable insolence
Of that proud Dame, the Lord Protectors Wife.
She invades the Court each day, with Troopes of Ladies,
And vanquishes my Glory so entirely,
That I appear a little falling Star,
And she a Comet upon whom all gaze.
Her very Habit does exceed in cost
Th' expences of a little Princes Court.
She Swim's along the Court, like a Guilt Ship,
New come from *India*, laden all with Jewels,
And then she scorns to strike her Sayl to me,
But over-looks me, like a little Pinke
Laden with Toyes and Fripperies from *France*.
This slave to Pride, that shou'd be slave to me,
Vaunted amongst her Minions the other day,
The very Train of her worst wearing Gown,
Was better worth then all my Fathers Lands,
Till *Suffolk* gave two Dukedoms for his Daughter.

Suff. Laugh

The MURDER of the D. of GLOCESTER.

Suff. Laugh at her Pride; for, Madam, it shall shortly
Be your Divertisement, and her Destruction.
I've dug a Pit for the fierce Lyoness.
Who, greedy of Honor, ranges to the very
Suburbs of Hell for it; and I've turn'd loose
Jackalls to tempt her to the Pit in shew,
Of guiding her to her desired Prey.
See here comes one of my Jackalls——Sir *John*
What News?

Enter Humes.

Humes. Good News, my Lord, I have been with the Duchess,
And did Salute her in the Devil's Name,
With the Title of Majesty.
  Suff. Ha! ha! ha!   (*Laughs.*)
  Qu. What do you mean?
  Suff. Madam, the Story will make you Laugh; the Duchess
Is going to the Devil for Preferment.
  Qu. How? To the Devil?
  Suff. Yes; and bribes this Gentleman,
To find out some of the Devil's Spyes and Agents,
To ayd her in a Correspondence with him.
  Humes. Madam, it is most true, and I've found out
One *Margery Jordan*, an experienc'd Witch,
And *Roger Bullingbrook* a Conjurer,
And they pretend they'l raise from Hell a Spirit
Shall tell her all she'l aske.
  Qu. Sure they are Cheats.
  Suff. They shall be Cheats to her, and her Duke *Humphry.*
Two mortal Devils, call'd *York* and *Buckingham*,
Shall send their Devil to Hell, and carry her
To what she more than Hell abhors, to shame
And ruine, and her Duke shall quickly follow:
He must have share of it in spite of him.
  Qu. Oh! my *La Poole*, that I were now in private   (*aside.*
To Kiss thee for this Plot! Oh! 'tis a rare one!
Humes, carry on this Plot, here's Gold for thee,
Thou shalt have more.
  Humes. So, the Gold tumbles in
On every side of me, but 'tis no wonder.   (*aside.*
I serve the Master of the Mines of the Devil,
And how in Hell he uses Slaves I know not:
He is an excellent Master in this World.   (*Exit.*
  Qu. Oh! *Suffolk!* thou didst never look so lovely
In all thy Life as now; nor did I ever

Feel such transporting pleasure in my Soul.
Now I shall be a Queen.

   Suff. A glorious one.
I'm sure the fairest *England* ever saw.

   Qu. Oh! *Suffolk!* bravest, loveliest of Men!
I'm trebly blest by thee, thou dost delight
My Love, and my Revenge, and my Ambition.
Now all the Ladies that in scorn of me,
Flatter'd and waited on proud *Gloster*'s Wife,
Shall suddenly repent their sawcy follies.

   Suff. The Duke's of *Somerset*, and *Buckingham*,
With the Insolent Cardinal, shall all fall too.
As for the Duke of *York*, this late Complaint
Will make but little for his benefit;
So one by one we'l tumble e'm all down.

   Qu. And on the Ruines of 'em all, we'l revel.

   Suff. And *England* at the Queen's command shall be.

   Qu. I'le Govern that, and thou shalt govern me.

ACT II.

The King and Queen sat in State, Duke Humphry, Cardinal, Buckingham, York, Salisbury, Warwick, and the Duchess attending.

   King. FOr my own part, my Lords, I care not whether
Rules *France*, the Duke of *Somerset*, or *York*,
All's one to me, they are both fitting Men.

   York. Sir, if I ill demean'd my self in *France*,
Then let me be deny'd the Regentship.

   Som. Sir, if I be unworthy of the place,
Then give the Duke of *York* the Regentship.

   War. Whether your Grace, my Lord, be worthy or not,
Dispute not that, the Duke of *York* is worthier.

   Car. Ambitious *Warwick!* let your betters speak.

   War. The Cardinal's not my betters in the Field.

   Buck. My Lord, all in this Presence are your betters.

   War. In Title, not in Fortune, or in Courage.

   Sal. Peace, Son!

   King. Oh! peace my Lords! Do not you know
What little pleasure I have in my Crown,
And Do you strive to make me wearier of it?
You take it ill if I refuse you Governments;

Yet

The MURDER of the D. of GLOCESTER.

Yet you deny to let me Rule in quiet.
I wonder what you see in this vile World
Worth the contending for. Heaven has entrusted me
With Three Great Kingdoms, *England, France* and *Ireland,*
And I must give Account of 'em to Heaven,
And not throw up my Charge for my own ease;
Else I wou'd gladly give e'm all to buy
The holy Peace, any of you may have.
Yet you disturb your selves and me for Rule,
Which I account a Pennance for my sins.

  Qu. Is this a King that speaks? or some poor Pilgrim,
That having lost his way, seates himself ignorantly
Down in a Throne, and does not know 'tis one.
And falls a Preaching to the gaping Multitude.
Oh! What a Prince is this to sway three Kingdoms?   (*Aside.*
And what a Husband's this for a young Queen?

  Yo. Most Gratious Soveraign! our chief contention
Is to give you that ease which you delight in,
To lay the burden of your Government
On Men whose Loyalty and great Abilities
May bear e'm up, both to your ease and glory.

  Sal. And for the Government of *France,* my Lord
Of *York,* no Man so fitting as your self.
And pray my Lord of *Buckingham,* shew reason
Why you prefer the Duke of *Somerset?*

  Qu. Because 'tis the King's Will to have it so.

  Glou. Madam, the King is old enough himself
To speak his Mind; these are no Womens matters.

  Qu. If he be old enough, What needs your Grace
To be Protector of His Majesty?

  Glou. Madam, I am Protector of the Kingdom,
And at His pleasure will resign my Place.

  Suff. Resign it then, and leave your Insolence;
Since you were King, (As who is King but you?)
The Common-wealth has daily run to ruine.
The Dauphin seiz'd our Provinces in *France,*
And you our Liberties and Honors here.

  Car. The Commons you have Rack't, the Clergies Bags
Are lank and lean with your Extortions.

  Som. You spend the Publick Treasure most profusely,
On Sumptuous Buildings for your Luxury,
And costly Attire for your Wive's Vanity.

  Elia. So! so! my Dress becomes a Crime of State;
Shortly I do believe you will Arraign
My Necklaces and Bodkins of High Treason;
You cannot do it by the Law of *England,*

'Cause they have not their Equals here to try 'em by.

 Buck. We may extort the Law as oft your Husband
Has done, to punish beyond bounds of Law.

 Qu. And not content to waste the Publick Treasure,
Both on his own, and his Wive's foolish Pride.
He has, as the Suspition's very strong,
Made Sale of Offices and Towns in *France*,
Which if 'twere prov'd, shou'd make him lose his Head.

 Glo. How am I baited beyond Human sufferance?
I will go out and coole, lest I be tempted
To act or speak any thing
Unworthy of my self, and of this Presence   (*Exit.*

 King. My Lords, my Lords, I see, and grieve to see
Too much Ill-mindedness in all this Fury.
We oft by Lightning read in darkest Night,
And by your Passions I read all your Natures,
Though you at other times can keep e'm dark;
But I have Read e'm when you thought it not,
And I my self scarce minded what I did.
I, like the musing *Hermit* in the Desert,
Feel the cold nipping blasts of the rough Wind,
And hear the Howles of Wolves, and Yelpes of Foxes,
Though I regard e'm not, nor mind at all
To shun e'm, or to fortifie against e'm.

 Card. I hope the King rankes not among the Wolves
One of the Shepherds of the Sacred Flock.

 King. I shou'd be glad I had no cause at all.

 Suff. I hope there's none of us has spoken any thing
But from deep sence of Loyalty and Honor
Against a Traytor to the King and Kingdom.

 King. I'le Judge so honourably of you all,
To think, you only eccho Publick Rumor;
And Ecchoes that miscall the Passenger
Injure him not, but they that set e'm talking.
Publick Report then wrongs the Duke, not you;
For if you know him false, Why don't you prove it?
Then you do ill, to do no more then Talke.

 Qu. Sir, subtle Men don't use to act their Wickedness
In Roades, in Markets, or on Steeple tops;
But closely hid; so hid, that oft the Devil
Who did employ e'm, scarce knows what they mean.

 Eliz. Come, Sir, all this is spoken out of envy,
Low crawling envy, envy that is chok'd
With the great Dust the Train of my Robes make.
Whence came this beggarly Spirit into *England* ?
It never can be of the English growth.

              The

The MURDER of the D. of GLOCESTER. 15

The late great Conquerors of Towns and Provinces
Fallen to envy a Lady's Cloaths? Oh! beggarly!
Some poor French Pedler brought this Spirit hither,
'Mongst the small Wares, they sell so dear to us.
    Qu. Oh! how she taunts me!——this is meant to me!   (*Aside.*
I will take an occasion to affront her.   (*Lets fall her Fan.*
Give me my Fan!—— What, Minion, Can you not?
                  She gives the Duchess a Box o'th' eare.
I cry you Mercy, Madam, Was it you?
    Elia. Yes, it was I, proud Daughter of a Beggar.
Strike me thy betters, many times thy betters,
Bating the Dignity the King bestows on thee.
No mar'le thou look'st with envy on my Jewels;
Thy Father cou'd not give thee Gold enough
Only to Guild one of the Kings Prayer-Books.
The King was forc'd to give him two great Provinces,
That so it might not shamefully be said,
The Father of the Queen of *England* starves.
    Qu. So! so!
    King. Fye Madam! Fye! this is too much
Pray Rule your self, it was against her will.
    Elia. Against her will? no! Sir! 'twas with her will,
And shortly she will do as much to you.
But she shall never strike me unreveng'd——   *Exit. Elia.*
    Buck. I will follow her my Lord Cardinal,
And listen after the Duke, how he proceeds.
The Duchess Fury now will need no spurs,
She'l gallop fast enough to her destruction.
    Card. And let her gallop, and the Devil speed her—— *Ex. Buck.*

Enter Duke Humphry.

    Glo. My Lords, I've walk'd away from all that passion,
Which your false spiteful Accusations
Had kindled in my breast; and now I come
In a cold candid temper to advise you
To spare your selves, for me you cannot hurt.
Bring any Proofs of what you have accused me,
And I lye open to the Law as any Man,
At least I will do so; for if you think
My Office fences me, I'le throw it down.
But to the matters that we have in hand,
I say the Duke of *York*'s the fittest person
To be your Regent Sir in *France*.
    Suff. Before Election's made, let me shew reason why
The Duke of *York* is most unfit of any Man.
                                     York. My

York. My Lord of *Suffolk,* I will tell you why,
Becaufe I fcorn to be your Flatterer.
Next, if I be appointed for the place,
Such is my Lord of *Somerfets* ambition
And hate to me, that he will keep me here,
Without Difcharge, Money, or Furniture,
Till *France* be wonn; he had rather it were loft,
Than any one fhou'd rule it but himfelf.
Laft time I danc'd Attendance on his will,
Till *Paris* was befieg'd, famifh'd, and loft.

War. That I can witnefs, and a blacker Treafon
Was ne'r committed——

Suff. Peace, my Lord of *Warwick!*
Here's one shall filence you, and him you plead for.

Enter Armorer *and his Man* Peter.

York. How? Silence me?

Suff. Yes; here is a Man accufed
Of Treafon, that relates to you my Lord.

York. Does any one accufe me for a Traytor?

King. What do you mean, my Lord? What Men are thefe?

Suff. An't pleafe your Majefty, this is the Man
That does Accufe his Mafter of High Treafon.
His words were thefe; That *Richard* Duke of *York*
Was the true lawful heir to the Crown of *England:*
And that your Majefty was an Ufurper.

King. Say Man, Were thefe thy words?

Arm. An't pleafe your Majefty,
I never faid, nor thought any fuch matter:
Heaven is my witnefs I am falfely accus'd.

Pet. By thefe ten bones, he fpoke e'm to me one night, my Lord in the Garret, when we were fcow'ring the Duke of *York's* Armour.

York. Bafe Villain! I will have thee hang'd for this
Moft Trayt'rous Speech.
I do befeech your Majefty,
Let him find all the rigour of the Law.

Ar. Hang me, my Lord, if ever I fpoke thefe words;
My Accufer is my Prentice, and I correcting him
For his Fault the other day, he Vow'd on's knees
He'd be reveng'd on me, I have good witnefs;
Therefore I befeech your Majefty, caft not away
An Honeft Man, for a Rogues Accufation.
One that has been a Rogue, Sir, all his Life,
A moft notorious Rogue, Sir, I befeech you.

King.

The MURDER of the D. of GLOCESTER.

King. Unckle, What shall we say to this in Law?
Glo. If I may Judge, Sir, let the Duke of *Somerset*
Be Regent o'r the French, because the Duke
Of *York* lies under violent suspition.
And let these have a day appointed e'm
For single Combate, 'cause the Armourer
Has Witness of his Servants Threats and Malice.
This is the Law, and this is, Sir, my Sentence.
King. Let it be so.
Som. I humbly thank your Majesty.
Armo. And I accept the Combat willingly.
Pet. Alass! my Lord, I cannot fight! oh! pity me!
Oh Heaven have mercy on me! I shall never
Be able to strike a blow! — oh! Lord! my heart! Why the
Devil must I fight? Is this my Reward for Witnessing? I cannot fight.
Glo. Sirrah! you must fight, or be hang'd.
King. Away with e'm to Prison! till the Combat.
Come, my Lord Duke, I will dispatch you to *France*.
All go out but the Cardinal.
Card. I will not rest till I've the Blood of *Glocester*:
He must be Lord Protector of the Kingdom,
And Lord it over me. He thinks he is
A better Man, 'cause he is a King's Son,
And I but Son of the Duke of *Lancaster*.
He is the Son of *Henry* the Fourth,
And I of *Henry*'s Father *John* of *Gaunt*.
But at my making there it seems did want
Some Holy Ceremonies, for want of which
I'm that the Rude Ill-manar'd Law calls Bastard.
And 'cause the Law has thrust me from Succession
To the great Temporal Glories of my Father,
They wrap'd me up in a Priest's Robe, and lay me
Out of the World; and in the way of Heaven.
They shou'd have drest poor *Henry* in this Child's Coat,
And laid him in the Cradle of the Church,
And hum'd him fast asleep with Holy Stories;
His little Soul was fitter for those things.
Well, I will go to Heaven; but in my way
I at the Lord Protectorship will bayt,
Or I will lye abroad in stormes of Blood.
My Cosins themselves Legitimate may call;
Their Souls compar'd with mine are Bastards all.   *Exit.*

Enter

Enter Elianor, Humes; *the Scene a Room in the Conjurer's House.*

Elia. Where are your Instruments?
Humes. They are both ready,
Preparing their dire Charms and Exorcisms.
Elia. Call e'm.

Enter Bullingbrook *and the Witch.*

Humes. Come in; this, Madam, is *Roger Bullingbrook*,
A Man of wonderful and dreadful Art;
He has a Key to the Infernal deep,
And let's abroad what Spirit he will, and when;
And when he will he Chains him up again.
This Woman equals him in Power and Art,
Her Name is *Jordan*.
Elia. Come, begin your Charmes.
Bull. Dare you be present, Madam?
Elia. Dare the Devil
Come in my presence? for I dare meet him.
Bull. Madam, you may, for Heaven fetters him,
And gives us Mortal Creatures Power to do so:
I gain'd my Art by Prayer, and profound Study;
Then nothing fear.
Elia. I ne'r knew what fear was.
Bull. Go, Mother *Jordan*, get the Incense ready. (*The Witch goes out.*
Elia. Well said, my Masters, come, begin, begin.
Bull. Pray Patience, Madam, for we know our times.
Our time is in the Deep, and Silent Night;
The time when Cities oft are set on fire;
When Robberies and Murders are committed;
When Bandogs Howle, and Shreich-Owles Warn the Dying;
When Spirits Walk, and Ghosts break up their Graves;
Then Devils come abroad to meet their Friends,
And that's the time best fit's our present Work:
But, Madam, sit, and fear not, whom we raise
We will make fast within a hallowed Verge.

Enter the Witch *with a Pan of Coales.*

Bull. Fling Incense in, then grovel on the Earth.
The Witch *fling's something on the Coales, and then the Conjurer immediately falls prostrate, makes a Circle with his Wand, then takes a Book and Reades.*

Bull.

The MURDER of the D. of GLOCESTER. 19

Bull. Thou mighty Spirit, one of the chief Powers
And Potentates in the Infernal Kingdom,
Whose Empire extends wide in Night and Chaos,
Whose Provinces are Peopled thick with damn'd;
By that Authority he gives me o'r thee,
Who hurl'd thee down into these doleful Regions,
I chargee thee to obey my dread Commands,
And at my calling to appear——Appear!——
Asmath appear!

Bull. } *Asmath*——Appear!——appear!——
Witch. }

      Thunder and Lightning, a Sprit rises.

 Spirit. I'm here!——
Bull. I charge thee by th' eternal being,
Whose name and power thou ever tremblest at:
To Answer that I Ask; for till thou speak
Thou shalt not stir from hence.
 Spirit. Ask what thou wilt——
But prethee do not keep me with thee long.
 Bull. First of the King: What shall become of him?
 Spirit. The Duke now lives, that *Henry* shall Depose;
But him out-live, and dye a violent Death.
 Bull. Now say, What fate attends the Duke of *Suffolk*?
 Spirit. By Water shall he meet his latest Breath.
 Bull. What shall befall the Duke of *Somerset*?
 Spirit. Let him shun Castles;
Safer shall he be on the Sandy Plains,
Then where Castles mounted stand.
H'a done, for more I hardly can endure.
 Bull. Descend to darkness, and the Burning Lake.
Be gon! be gon!——
    The Spirit descends with Thunder and Lightning.

 Enter the Dukes of York *and* Buckingham *with a Guard, and seize e'm.*
 Yo. Lay hands upon these Traytors, and their Trash.
 Elia. Ha!
 Yo. Madam, yes, I think we have watch'd you narrowly;
The King and Kingdom are indebted to you
For this fine piece of Work: my Lord Protector,
Who, no doubt, set you a Work, will see you rewarded.
 Elia. What mighty Mischief have I done, my Lords?
Talked with a Devil? I every day converse
With worse then Devils, with your selves, my Lords.
But I've it seems disturb'd the Peace of Hell;
What, you have Interest there? and many Friends!
     D 2   Forgive

Forgive me, Lords, but yet you can disturb
The King and Kingdom's Peace; Is that no Crime?
 Buck. You have commited, Madam, then no crime
It seems ——away with thoſe, and Guard e'm cloſe;
Keep e'm aſunder; ſee that all their Trinkets
Be forth-coming ———Madam, you muſt with us.
     Guard lead out Elia. Witch *and* Conjurer.
 Yo. This was an excellent Plot, well choſe t' build on.
Now pray my Lord let's ſee the Devil's Writ.
The Duke yet lives, that *Henry* ſhall Depoſe;   (*Reads.*
But him outlive, and dye a violent death.
 Buck. This is juſt *Aio te Æacida Romanos vincere poſſe.*
 Yo. The Devil ſtill keeps to his old trade of Quibling.
 Buck. He is the Father of all Lyers and Quiblers.
 Yo. Well to the reſt.
What Fate attends the Duke of *Suffolk?*   (*Reads.*
By Water ſhall he meet his lateſt breath.
What ſhall befall the Duke of *Somerſet?*
Let him ſhun Caſtles:
Safer ſhall he be on Sandy Plains,
Then where Caſtles mounted ſtand.
Fine ſtuff——The Devil I ſee is grown old and dull.
The King is now in Progreſs towards St. *Albans,*
With him the Husband of this lowly Lady.
Whether go all theſe Cloudy Oracles
Asfaſt as Horſe can carry e'm———
A ſorry Breakfaſt for my Lord Protector.
 Buck. Your Grace ſhall give me leave my Lord of *York*
To be the Poſt.
 Yo. My Lord, at your own pleaſure.
Within there ho!

     Enter a Servant.

Intreat my Lords of *Salisbury* and *Warwick*
To take a ſhort Collation at my Houſe
This Afternoon, away: My Lord your Servant——*Ex.*

  Enter the King, Queen, Protector, Cardinal, Suffolk, *as from*
   Hawking. *Attendants,* Somerſet, Salisbury, Warwick.

 Qu. Believe me, Lords, for flying at the Brook
I ne'r had better ſport in all my life.
Yet by your leave the Wind was very high.
 King. But what a Point, my Lord, your Falcon made?
And what a pitch ſhe flew above the reſt.
              Suff. My

The MURDER of the D. of GLOCESTER.

Suff. My Lord Protector's Hawks towre like their Master,
Above their Fellows.
 Glo. 'Tis an humble Mind
That mounts, my Lord, no higher than a Bird.
 Card. I thought he soon wou'd be above the Clouds.
 Gl. Ay, my Lord Cardinal, how think you by that?
Wou'd not your Grace be glad to mount towards Heaven?
 K. The Treasury of Everlasting Joy.
 Card. Your Heaven is on Earth, your eyes and thoughts
Beat on a Crown, the Treasure of your Heart,
Pernitious, haughty, treacherous Protector!
Who smooth it thus both with the King and Kingdom.
 Gl. How, Cardinal!
Tantæ e animis Cœlestibus iræ! Church-Men so hot?
Uncle, for shame let your Robe hide your Malice.
 Suff. No Malice, my Lord, but Zeal, that which becomes
So good a Quarrel, with so bad a Lord.
 Gl. As who?
 Suff. Why, as your Self, my Lord Protector.
 Gl. My Lord of *Suffolk*, *England* knows your Insolence.
 Qu. And your Ambition, my Lord of *Glocester*.
 K. How, Madam! You a Stirrer of Debate?
These are the pleasant Sounds that follow me
Where-e'er I go: I'm an Inchanted Isle,
Surrounded with Eternal raging Storms,
Whoe'er approaches me, hazards a Wreck:
These Winds and Waves beat on my Lord Protector,
Because he is a Rock that Guards my Coast.
 Card. Good Heaven, what Arts has the Protector us'd
To charm you, Sir, that you can see all Loyalty
In him who means you hurt? and none in us,
Who shew our Loyal Zeal to guard you from him?
Were it but one of us that shewed this Zeal,
It might be thought an Envy to his Greatness,
And a design to get into his Office:
But since we all unite our Accusations,
We can have no design but Loyalty,
Since all of us cannot be Lord Protectors.
 K. But all may hope, though only one can be so.
But come, my Lords, do not I know you all?
I mind you often, when you think I do not.
You think I'm fast asleep to all this World,
I wou'd be so, but you disturb my rest,
And break my slumbers with your furious Broils,
And make me mind you whether I will or no.
Alas, I pity you, you wrong your selves

Much

Much more than me; and yet you trouble me,
Trouble my Counsels, trouble my Devotions,
Trouble my Sports; but, Sirs, I thank you for it,
For by these Tempests you stir up the Mud
That lodges in the bottom of this World,
And make all Pleasures here a Puddle to me,
And make me long for the pure Joys above,
To do me good, though you design me none.
 Qu. Here I am tir'd with everlasting Preaching.   *(Aside.*
 Card. The King and I ought to change Offices,   *(Aside.*
He is more fit to be a Priest than I,
And I'm more fit to be a King than he:
Thus Crowns and Mitres are at random thrown,
And very seldom light on Heads that fit 'em.

Enter one crying a Miracle.

 Gl. What means this noise?
 One. A Miracle! A Miracle!
 Car. What Miracle? An Usurer made charitable?
A Lawyer honest, or a Courtier faithful,
A Woman constant, or a Souldier godly?
 Suff. Come to the King, and tell him, Friend, what Miracle.
 One. Forsooth a Blind Man at St. *Albans* Shrine,
Within this half hour has receiv'd his sight,
A Man that ne'er saw in his life before.
 Suff. That's a strange Miracle indeed, my Friend.
 K. Th' Eternal Goodness, and Omnipotence,
Be prais'd, for all thy wondrous Works to Men;
He has not only given this poor man sight,
But by this miracle given light to truth.
 Card. I will be hang'd, if this be not some damn'd cheat *(Aside.*
Plaid by the Fryars: I who wait at the Altar,
Know well what tricks are plaid behind the Altar,
Yet I must countenance it with a grave look,
But 'tis strange truth that stands in need of lyes.
Well, Heaven be prais'd, Sir, for this miracle;   *(To the K.*
Here come the Fryars and Townsmen on Procession,
To present your Majesty with the man.

Enter Abbot, Fryars, Mayor of St. Albans, *and his Brethren, bearing the Man in a Chair, his Wife with him.*

 Gl. Stand by, my Masters, bring him near the King,
It is his Majesties pleasure to talk with him.
 K. Good Fellow, tell us all the circumstances,

That

The MURDER of the D. of GLOCESTER.   23

That all of us may glorifie Heaven for thee.
Wert thou born blind?
  Simp. Born blind, an't pleafe your Grace.
  Wife. I indeed was he forfooth.
  Suff. What Woman's this?
  Wife. His Wife, an't like your Worfhip.
  Gl. If thou hadft been his Mother, thou cou'dft better
Have told.
  Suff. What thinks your Majefty of this?   (*To the Qu.*
  Qu. Some trick o' the Fryars to cheat the filly people: (*Afide.*
They are all a pack o' Rogues.
  Suff. Oh! damn'd Rogues all.   (*Afide.*
  K. Where wert thou born?
  Simp. At *Berwick*, an't pleafe your Grace.
  Suff. So far in the North, and come hither for Cure?
What, was there ne'er a Northern Saint to help thee?
No Saint in *Scotland?*
  Simp. Not that I e'er heard of:
I never heard of any Saint in *Scotland,*
An't like your Worfhip.
  Suff. Truly nor I neither.
  Qu. There is a Saint in *Wales,* Saint *Winifrid,*
Many miles nearer *Berwick* than Saint *Albans,*
Why didft not go to her? She's a good Saint,
And does abundance of good Offices.
  Simp. She is fo, an't pleafe you forfooth Madam,
I've heard of her, but fhe is fo full of bufinefs,
Does fo many Cures for Englifh, Welfh, and Irifh;
That I was loath to trouble the good Lady:
Befides, I was afraid fhe wou'd not be
At leifure a great while to look to me,
And I did long to get a little fight forfooth.
  K. Poor Soul, Heaven's goodnefs has been great to thee,
Heaven has open'd a new gate of comforts to thee,
Shewed thee the richeft brighteft half of time,
Turn'd o'er the guilded leaves of Natures Book,
Where thou fhalt read things thou cou'dft ne'er imagine,
Coyn all this golden time in praife and prayer,
And thou fhalt find too at this gate of fight,
Armies of new temptations enter in,
Therefore ftand more than ever upon thy Watch.
  Card. How this tale finks into the King's foft Soul!   (*Afide.*
A Cannon cou'd not fhoot it into mine;
Yet I muft face this fable with my Scarlet,
To make it pafs for the Honour of the Church.
Upon fuch Legs as thefe the poor Church halts,

                Though

Though we conceive it's halting with our Robes.

Qu. Tell me, good Fellow, cam'st thou here by chance,
Or out of pure Devotion to this Shrine?

Simp. Indeed forsooth out of most pure Devotion,
Being call'd I'm confident a hundred times,
And oftner in my sleep by good Saint *Albans*.

Suff. How didst thou know it was Saint *Albans* call'd thee?

Simp. He said he was Saint *Albans*, if it please you.

Suff. He told thee in thy sleep so?

Simp. Yes, an't please you.

Suff. What said Saint *Albans*?

Simp. He said, *Saunder*, an't please your Worship,
Come, offer at my Shrine, and I will help thee:
Come, *Saunder*, come.

Wife. Indeed 'tis true forsooth,
For many a time and oft my self have heard
A voice to call him so.

Suff. What in thy sleep?

Wife. No forsooth, waking, as I'm now forsooth.

Suff. Friend, thou wert much in good Saint *Albans* favour.

Simp. I truly, I am much beholding to him.

Card. What, art thou lame?

Simp. Yes, Heaven help me, Sir. *Suff.* How cam'st thou so?

Simp. By a fall from a Tree.

Wife. Yes, he fell down from a high Plum-tree, Master.

Gl. Wert thou born blind, and yet wouldst climb a tree?

Simp. Never but once, and then my Wife desired me
To get some Damsons for her, and I cou'd not
Deny her any thing, I lov'd her dearly, she's a good Wife forsooth.

Card. Alas, good Couple.

Gl. This is a Rogue, and I'll discover him: *(Aside.*
Let me see thine eyes:——wink now; now open 'em:
In my opinion yet thou seest not well.

Simp. Yes, Master, clear as day, I thank St. *Albans*.

Gl. Sayst thou me so? What colour is that Gown?

Simp. Red, Master, Red as Blood.

Gl. Why, that's well said.
What colour is my Hat?

Simp. Black, Black forsooth, Coal-black as Jet forsooth.

K. Why, then thou know'st what colour Jet is of?

Suff. And yet he ne'er saw Jet in all his life.

Gl. But Gowns and Hats before this day good store.

Wife. Never before this day in all his life.

Gl. What's my Name, Sirrah?

Simp. Master, I know not.

Gl. What is his Name?

Simp.

The MURDER of the D. of GLOCESTER.

Simp. Indeed I know not, Master.
Glo. No?
Simp. No indeed.
Glo. Nor his?
Simp. No truly Master.
Glo. What's thy own Name? Can'st thou tell that?
Simp. My Name is *Saunder Sympcox*, if it please you Master.
Glo. Then *Saunder Sympcox*, you are a Cheating Rogue.
f you had been born blind, you might as well
Have known our Names, as all the Names of Colours.
Sight may distinguish Colours, but not Name 'em.
St. *Albans* here, my Lords, has done a Miracle;
What if I do one, and restore this Cripple
To his Legs again?
Simp. Oh! Master! that you cou'd.
Suff. How came St. *Albans* did not cure thy Lameness
As well as Blindness?
Simp. Nay, I know not, Master.
Suff. Has he not Skill in Legs as well as eyes?
Simp. Yes, surely, Master, they are all one to him.
Suff. What he forgot e'm then?
Simp. I know not, Master;
If it had pleas'd him to have Cur'd my Legs,
I shou'd ha' been most mightily behold to him.
Glo. I'le ease him of that trouble, I will Cure thee.
Simpl. Ah, Master, that you cou'd.
Glo. I'le do't I say:
Have you no Beadles Mr Mayor? and things call'd Whips?
Mayor. Here is the Beadle, please your Grace.
Glo. I see a Stool there, bring it hither quickly.
Now, Sirrah, if you mean to save your self
From Whipping, leap o'r this Stool and run away.
Simp. Alass! Master, I am not able to stand alone;
You go about to Torture me in vain.
Glo. Well, Sirrah, I must have you find your Legs:
Whip him till he leap o'r that same Stool.
Simp. Master, What shall I do? I cannot stand.
Glo. Leap Sirrah! Leap!
Simp. Oh! oh!——
    Beadle *Whips him, he leaps over the Stool, and runs away,*
        and they cry a Miracle, follow.
King. Do'st thou behold this Heaven? and bear thus long?
Glo. Bring back the Rogue, and take this Drabbe away.
Wife. Alass! we did it for pure need, forsooth.
Glo. Let e'm be Whipt through every Market Town,
Till they come to *Berwick*, from whence they came.

E   *Car.*

Car. Heark you, Are not you a Company of Damn'd Fools
To employ such a Silly Rogue as this? (*Softly to a* Fryer.
That has shewn all your Cheats to the whole World?

Fry. My Lord, they were known to all Wise Men before;
And such a Fool will serve to Couzen Fools:
And Fools are those that we must hope to stand by. (*Exit.*

Enter Buckingham.

King. What Tidings brings my Lord of *Buckingham?*
Buc. Such as my heart does tremble to relate:
My Lord Protector's Wife has practis'd horridly,
And dangerously against your Majesties Life ———
H'as dealt with Hellish Conjurers and Witches
To raise up wicked Spirits from under Ground
To acquaint her with your destiny, and Councel her
How she may ayd your Fate, and hasten it.
She's enquir'd too of the Infernal Oracle
The Fates of several of your Majesties Council;
We apprehended e'm all in the Fact.

Car. Ha! Is she fallen into our Trap? that's well! — (*Aside.*
And she shall soon pluck her Duke *Humphrey* after.
My Lord Protector, your good Lady finding
She governs you, thinks she can rule the Devil,
And have th'infernal Powers at her Command.
Heaven be Prais'd, *England*'s Protected well.
Your Grace is Lord Protector of the Kingdom,
Your Wife rules you, the Devil is her Protector,
And so the Devil is *England*'s Lord Protector;
I hope we shall displace his Devilship.

Glo. And put a worse Devil in if you succeed.
But these good Churchmen are the heavenly comforts
You give your Kinsman in affliction.
You may insult, for sorrow has so vanquisht me,
The basest Groom may trample on me now.

King. What horrid things are practis'd in this World?
How vile ones heap confusion on their heads?

Qu. My Lord, my Lord, you see your nest is tainted;
Look that your self be faultless you had best.

Glo. Madam, I will not answer for a Woman:
For my own self, to heaven I appeal,
Who knowes how I have lov'd my King and Country.
And for my Wife, I know not how it stands,
Sorry I am to hear what I have heard.
Noble she is, but if she have forgot
Honor and Vertue, I will forget her,

And

The MURDER of the D. of GLOCESTER.

And banish her my Bed, and my Acquaintance;
And give her up to the just punishment
Which she deserves for so much wickedness,
And so dishonouring my honest Name.

King. I will to *London* with what haste I can,
To look into this business thoroughly,
And call these foul offenders to their Answers.
(*Ex. Om. præ.* Suff. *and the* Qu.

Qu. My dear, dear *Suffolk,* how thou every moment
Heap'st new delights on me? when thou didst get for me
The *English* Crown, thou didst not please me more,
Then now in getting me revenge on *Elianor.*
Treading on her, methinks I walk in Triumph
To a second and more pleasing Coronation.

Suff. I told you, Madam, I had snares for her.
You were impatient and cou'd not stay
Till things cou'd ripen.

Qu. Oh! thou art my Sun:
My joyes and glories ripen, grow and flourish
Under thy beautiful and glorious beams.
Come lets go see Dame *Elianor* in her shame,
The pleasing'st sight in the whole World, next thee.

Suff. Next sight I'le shew you, shall be *Gloster*'s fall;
The good fond Husband will be loth to stay
Behind his Wife, though she goes to destruction.

Qu. Sure thou wert made o' purpose for my Love;
Had heaven bid me ask for some great Merit,
A Gift that might have shewed bounty divine,
I wou'd have said, Let *Suffolk* heaven be mine.—— (*Ex.*

ACT III.

Enter York, Salisbury, *and* Warwick.

The SCENE the Duke of *York*'s House, long Scrowles lying on a Table.

York. Now my good Lords of *Salisbury* and *Warwick,*
You have perus'd my Title to the Crown,
I pray deliver me both your opinions.

War. My Lord, 'tis very plain, the Right is yours;
King *Henry* claimes the Crown from *John of Gaunt,*

Fourth Son of *Edward* the Third; Your Grace claims it
From *Lyonell* Duke of *Clarence* the Third Son:
Till *Lyonell*'s Issue fails, his shou'd not Reign.
It failes not yet, but flourishes in you,
And in your Sons, fair Branches of your Stock.
My Lord of *Salisbury* kneel we together,
And in this private Room be we the first
That shall Salute our Lawful Soveraign,
With the honor of his Birth-right to the Crown.

  Both. Long live our Sovereign, *Richard* King of *England.*
  York. My Lords, I give you both my hearty thanks;
But I am not your King till I be Crown'd,
And my Sword stayn'd in the heart blood of all
The House of *Lancaster*; and that's not suddenly,
Nor very easily to be perform'd:
We must use Counsel, Secresy, and Courage:
Do you as I do in these dangerous days,
Wink at the Duke of *Suffolk*'s Insolence;
At *Beauford*'s Pride; at *Somerset*'s Ambition;
At *Buckingham*, and all the Crew of e'm,
Till they have snar'd the good and wise Duke *Humphry*,
Whose Vertues are so many Guardian Angels
Both to the King and Kingdom; his destruction
These ill Men seek, and they in seeking that
Shall find their own, if I can Prophesie.

  Sal. My Lord, let us break off, we know your Mind.
  War. There's something great within my breast that tells me,
The Day is coming, when the Earl of *Warwick*
Shall make the Duke of *York* the King of *England.*

  Yo. And I shall live to make the Earl of *Warwick*
The greatest Man in *England* but the King ——   *Exit.*

The SCENE the Court.

Enter King and Queen, Duke of Suffolk, *Duke of* Glocester,
Cardinal, Elianor *a Prisoner.*

  King. Madam, stand forth, and hear your Sentence from me:
In sight of heaven and me your guilt is great;
A Crime, to which heavens Book adjudges Death:
Your Fellow Criminals shall suffer Death;
And 'tis notorious false reasoning
You shou'd be spar'd, because you are great and Noble;
The World is us'd to such false Reasonings,
And that's the cause there is so little Truth in it.

But

The MURDER of the D. of GLOCESTER.

But I obferve but few of the World's Cuftoms,
Nor will I now be lead away in this.
Then hear my Sentence; fince to your great Spirit
There is no pain like fhame; I Sentence you
To bear the tort'ring fhame of open Pennance:
And fince to live depos'd of all your Honors
In fome remote fad defolate obfcurity,
Is to you pain like burying alive,
I Sentence you to fpend your days in Banifhment
With Sir *John Stanley* in the Ifle of *Man*.

 Elia. Welcome my Banifhment; for I am fure
My doleful days will not be many there.

 Glo. Oh Wife! What haft thou brought upon thy felf?
Did not I timely warn thee of Ambition;
And fay, one day 'twou'd do fome difmal deed?
The King has paft a righteous Sentence on thee;
And none have reafon to complain but I,
Who innocently fuffer in thy fhame:
My honor fhares in all thy fad reproach,
And my love fuffers in thy Banifhment,
That I am punifh'd equally with thee,
Though I am innocent; and yet the King
Does me no wrong at all: no *Elianor*,
I've reafon to complain of none but thee,
Who woud'ft not take the Counfels that I gave thee,
Out of dear Love to thee.

 Elia. I fee my folly.

 Glo. Now haft thou brought difhonor on my age,
And fhame and grief will fink me to my Grave.

 Qu. My Lord, my Lord, you can be fenfible
Of your Wive's fhame; but not of the difhonor
The King and I both fuffer'd by her Infolence.
You weep, 'caufe fhe muft fuffer an hours Pennance;
But fhe has made me fuffer horrid Pennance
E'er fince I was her Queen, both to my own,
And the King's fhame and grief, that you ne'r wept for.
She muft walk barefoot now upon the ftones:
Time was, fhe trod on me, I was her way;
Which I endur'd to the King's fhame and mine:
And you for that had very fmall regret.

 Gl. Madam, if for her Crimes, her too great Crimes,
The punifhment the King has doom'd her to
Be not enough, pray Sentence her to more:
But let her know an end of punifhment.
But if the Scale be full enough already,

As the just King, who poiz'd it well, conceives;
Do not be heaping till it grows injustice.

  Qu. My Lord, she deserves more then she shall suffer;
Only for the intolerable rudeness
Wherewith she treated me her Queen to day;
To call me to my Face a Beggars Daughter?
Suppose I were that miserable Beggar,
Is it well done to tread on Poverty?
But when by Birth heaven made me a great Princess,
And the King's Love made me a great Queen, her Queen;
For her to treat me so? Was that well done?

  Suff. Yes, Madam, 'twas well done for his Designs
Of making her your Queen, your Majesty her subject:
That they had such Designs, her present Crimes
Are a sufficient proofe; and they did well
To bring you to subjection by degrees.

  Car. All the reflection I shall make is this;
He who was Govern'd by so ill a Woman,
Is very unfit to be the Kingdoms Governor;
She was his Counsellor, the Devil hers;
Conjecture then what his Designs must be.

  Glo. Lord Cardinal, I am sure of your good Word;
I see what all of you thirst for, my ruine.
I had long since remov'd out of your way,
If duty to my King had not detain'd me:
I was afraid to trust him in your hands,
But I perceive my stay occasions him
Perpetual trouble; and the heavenly power
Has an especial eye to Sacred Kings.
To his Protection then I'le leave the King,
If the King will permit me, and retire
To bear the heavy burden of my griefs.

  Qu. Pray do, my Lord, we'l take you at your word.
I see no reason, why a King of years
Shou'd be Protected like a little Child:
Resign your Staffe, and give the King his Kingdom,
The King by heaven's help may Govern it.

  King. Do, do my Lord, since they'l all have it so,
I shall not want a Counsel, or Protection,
For heaven is my hope, my stay, my guide.
And go in peace, less powerful, less great;
No less belov'd, by me, and all good Men.

Enter

The MURDER of the D. of GLOCESTER.

Enter York.

Glo. Then here, most Sacred Sovereign, is my Staffe;
As willingly do I resign it to you,
As e're your glorious Father made it mine.
As willingly lay it at your feet,
As others wou'd ambitiously receive it.
Farewell, good King, may you, when I am dead,
Never have cause to shed one tear for me.
When is your Royal Pleasure that my Wife
Shall do her Pennance?
King. Now, immediately.
Glo. Come, *Elianor*, let us support our Sorrows;
Sorrow is natural to this Vale of Tears.
My fall will rather pleasure to me bring,
If it shall cause no sorrow to the King.
(*Exit Glocester, Elianor with a Guard.*
King. Oh Lords, you have made me part with a good Man!
I wish I may never have need of him.
York. How? Has the Duke resign'd the Government?
Qu. Yes; *Henry* now is King; and I am Queen;
And *Humphry* Duke of *Glocester* scarce himself:
Two of his stately Branches are lopt from him;
His Wife is Banish'd, and his Staffe resign'd,
And he will shortly wither with the Mayme.
Yo. As I wou'd wish: How have these haughty Lords   (*aside.*
Most subtilly wrought their own destruction?
For now the King lies open to my Sword;
But they shall perish with him for their Villanies.

A Shout: Enter Buckingham.

King. Now! What's the News?
Buck. May it please your Majesty,
The Combate 'tween the *Armourer* and his *Man*,
The Appellant, and Defendant has been fought,
According as your Majesty appointed:
Truth has prevail'd; the Guilty *Armourer*,
Worsted by his Servant, has confest the Treason.
King. Where is the Fellow?
Buc. They are both without.
Come in———

Enter

Enter Armorer *and his Man with a Guard.*

King. What, Fellow, did you speak the words?
Arm. Yes, please your Majesty.
King. Yet you deny'd 'em.
Ar. I was unwilling to be hang'd an't please you.
King. But not unwilling to destroy thy Soul,
By spilling of an innocent Fellows blood,
As thou hast done, if right had not prevail'd.

Buck. Sir, it was right indeed that did prevail;
I never saw poor Fellow so afraid,
As the *Armorer's* Servant was in all my life,
And yet he beate his Master by his Innocence.

Arm. It was my Conscience beate me, and not he;
If my own Conscience had not fought against me,
I cou'd have beaten twenty such as he.

Pet. I do not know that, for though I was afraid
E're I came to it, now I know what it is,
I do not care if I have t'other bout.

King. There's mischief in this Business, I discern it; (*Aside.*
The Common People have been tamper'd with,
To try how they will like a change of Princes;
And to make way for it, my right is question'd,
And my good Lord Protector sent away from me.
Oh! heaven, if I be useful to my People,
Preserve me, for their sakes, from wicked Men;
If I be not, extend thy Providence
To them, and let what will become of me.
——— Go lead that Traytor to the Death he merits,
Thou honest man, whose truth and innocence
Heaven has reveal'd, by me shall be rewarded.

Exit Omnes præ. Suffolk *and the* Queen.

Qu. Now it goes excellently well indeed!
This haughty Woman tumbled in the dirt,
So far beneath my feet I cannot tread upon her.
Duke *Humphrey's* charming Rod broken in pieces;
Wherewith he kept, as in a Conjurers Circle,
The King and Kingdom both out of our reach.

Suff. Did not I promise you there shou'd be nothing
In *England*, Madam, that your Soul cou'd wish for
I'd not make yours?

Qu. And thou hast kept thy Word.
Suff. I think I promis'd you, that wonderful,
That ravishing moment, when I first beheld you,
When Fortune prodigally propitious to me,

With

The MURDER of the D. of GLOCESTER. 33

With Lawrels crown'd my Sword, my Arms with Beauty.
Flung Captive in my Arms such wondrous Beauty,
That when I saw it, I cry'd out amaz'd,
Our thundring Canons sure, has tore the Heavens,
And through the Chrystal breach, an Angel's dropt.

Qu. And I, when first I saw brave *Suffolk* shining
In Armour Victory, but most of all
In his own Charms! Oh! said I to my self,
I'le wonder now no more the English Conquerors,
They are Angels all, or Angels fight for 'em.

Suff. I most unworthy to support so bright
A Heaven of Beauty, did retire to gaze,
Whilst all my Soul came crowding to my eyes,
And thrusted till it almost crackt the Windows;
Then like a laden Thief, that stole more Wealth
Than he cou'd spend in all his Life, runs back
And lock't it up secure in every Room.

Qu. In vain is this rich guilding of that hour,
Which only was the portal of our Loves.
Since we are enter'd, and possess the Palace,
How I then wonder'd, and how since I lov'd,
Let all the Gardens, Groves, and happy Rooms,
That have been aiding to our Pleasures, tell.
So full of Life and Soul our Joys have been,
We have almost scatter'd Life to all things round us.
A thousand times I've thought the wanton Pictures,
Have striven to leap out of their Golden Frames
That held 'em Captive, and come share with us.
A thousand times, methought, I've seen their Mouths
Striving to break the painted shadows Bonds,
That held 'em bound in everlasting silence,
And burst into a Laughter, and a Rapture.

Suff. I never minded Pictures, when a Substance
Of so much Beauty lay in my embraces;
Nor *Venus*'s Picture, no nor *Venus*'s self,
Cou'd have extracted a regard from me.

Qu. How often has our Love in Groves and Gardens
Fill'd every Creature near us with such Spirit,
That they have danc'd to Death as they were stung;
The Birds have chirp'd their little souls away,
The Turtles bill'd till they have no breath;
The Winds have sported wantonly around us,
Till they have swoun'd away into a Calm.

Suff. Yet all this Love and Beauty which cou'd make
The sapless trunk of a dead Tree to bud,
Can put no warmth into the frozen King.

F *Qu.* Oh

Qu. Oh! to my Arms! He comes like depth of Winter,
With Cheeks all moist with Penitential Tears,
And Lips so cold, each kiss gives me an Ague.

Suff. Alas! How shou'd you expect them otherwise?
He comes from kissing Brazen Images,
And Bones, and Sculs of Saints, that were more cold
When they were living, than you'l be when dead.

Qu. Well, next to Love, Revenge has sweetest taste,
Let us go take some private stand, and see
Dame *Elianor* in her ridiculous Pomp
Walking the Streets, in her White Garment barefoot,
Holding a burning Torch to light her shame;
A gaping Crowd, and throng of hooting Boys
Following her Train, and the Belconies fill'd
With laughing Ladies, whom she onc'd contemn'd. (*A shout.*
Heark! they are coming, let's not loose the Pleasure. *Exit.*

The SCENE a Street.

Enter Duke Humphry, *and his Men in Mourning Cloaks.*

Gl. Oh! What a Change is here in my condition?
Fallen from the highest Pinacle of Glory,
Down to the lowest depth of Shame and Ruine.
From being Ruler of the King and Kingdom,
To be the Scorn and Sport of common Fellows.
Oh! *Elianor!* I've wrong'd my self and thee
By doting on thee, beyond bounds of Reason.
Thy Errors did appear to me all Excellencies.
But thou poor *Nell*, hast punishment enough,
I'le not heap more on thee by my Complaints.
Alas! how will thy tender Feet endure
To kiss the rugged face of cutting Flints?
How hardly will thy noble Spirit brook
The abject People gazing on thy Face,
With scornful looks deriding thy Disgrace,
Who lately followed thy proud shining Chariot,
And did not care what dirt the Wheels flung on 'em,
Might they be blest out with a look from thee. (*A shout.*
But soft! I think she come's! and I'le prepare
My Tear-stain'd Eyes, to see her Miseries.

Serv. So, please your Grace, we'll force her from the Sheriff.

Gl. No, stir not for your lives, she shall submit
To what the King was pleas'd t' inflict upon her.

Ente

The MURDER of the D. of GLOCESTER.

Enter the Duchess *in a White Sheet, a Taper burning in her Hand,* Sheriff, *and* Officers.

El. Come you, my Lord, to see my open shame?
Can you endure it? If you have no sense
Of my great Sufferings, pity your self,
For you in seeing my shame do Penance with me.
See how the gaping Multitude all point
And nod their Heads, and throw their Eyes on you.
Ah! my Lord! hide you from their odious looks,
And shut up in your Closet, mourn my shame,
And curse mine Enemies, both mine and yours.
 Gl. Be patient gentle *Nell*, forget this grief.
 El. First teach me to forget my self and you;
For whilst I think I am your Wife, and you
A Prince, and Lord Protector of the Kingdom,
Methinks this shou'd not be my Garb, and Pomp,
I shou'd not thus be lead along the Streets
Wrapt up in shame, with Papers on my Back,
And followed by a Rabble, that rejoyce
To see my Tears, and hear my deep-fetch'd Groans.
The pitiless Flints gash deep my tender Feet,
And when I start, the envious People laugh,
And bid me be advised how I tread.
 Gl. What if they do, my Love? What matter is it?
They do but shew their low degenerate natures.
Wert thou condemn'd into a Wilderness,
Would'st thou expect to have the Tygers court thee,
The Lions flatter thee, wild Beasts adore thee;
These Crowds are little better, little gentler.
 El. Oh! I cannot endure this heavy shame,
My Soul boyls under it, and my Heart breaks.
I never will behold the Sun again;
Nor face of Humane Creature! Dark obscurity,
Where never eye of Man, nor voice of Fear
Can penetrate, shall cover me for ever,
Out of the sight and memory of the World,
And bury all the World too out of mind.
Nay, if Love will not be too hard for me,
I will not let thee come into my mind.
For, oh! what deadly sorrow will it breed,
To think I am the Duke of *Glocester*'s Wife.
And he a Prince and Governour of *England*
Yet so he Rul'd, and such a Prince he was,
As he stood by, whilst his forlorn Duchess

F 2 Was

Was made a Wonder and a Pointing-ſtock
To every idle raſcal follower.

Gl. What wou'dſt thou have me do?

El. Nay, nothing, nothing,
Be mild, and tame, and bluſh not at my ſhame,
Be ſtirr'd at nothing, 'till the Ax of Death
Fall on thy ſelf, as ſhortly ſure it will.
For *Suffolk*, he that can do all in all,
With that vile Woman, who abhors us all;
And *York*, and impious *Beauford*, that falſe Prieſt;
Have all laid Snares, which thou ſhalt never ſcape.
But fear not thou, until thy Foot be ſnar'd,
Nor ever ſeek prevention of thy Enemies,
Till thou art fallen lower than I am now.

Gl. Ah! *Nell*, forbear, for now thou aim'ſt awry,
I muſt offend before I can be hurt;
And had I twenty times ſo many Enemies,
And each of e'm had twenty times their power,
Not all of e'm cou'd work me any damage
So long as I am Loyal, True, and Faultleſs:
But thou wou'd'ſt have me reſcue thee from ſhame;
I cannot do it, from theſe Officers
If I ſhou'd force thee, I can ne're redeem thee
From th' everlaſting Scandal that will follow thee.
Thy greateſt help is quiet, then ſweet *Nell*;
I pray thee fort thy heart with patience.

Enter a Herald.

Her. I ſummon your Grace to his Majeſties Parliament
Holden at *Bury*, the firſt of this next Month.

Gl. And my conſent ne're ask'd herein before?
This is cloſe dealing. Well, I will be there.   (*Ex. Herald.*

El. Lo you my Lord! What think you now?

Gl. I think
My Love as thou doſt, Miſchief is deſign'd me.
But if my Innocence will not protect me,
Guilt ſhall not do it; I will keep my Loyalty
Whilſt I can keep my Life.

El. Oh! that I fear
Will not be long.

Gl. Well, Heaven's will be done.
Love, I muſt take my leave; and Maſter Sheriff,
Let not her Penance exceed the King's Commiſſion.

Sher. An't pleaſe your Grace, here my Commiſſion ſtay's:
And Sir *John Stanly* is appointed now,
To take her with him to the Iſle of *Man*.   *Stanly*,

The MURDER of the D. of GLOCESTER.

Stanly. So am I given in charge, an't please your Grace.
Gl. Pray use her well, the World may smile again,
And I may live to return any Kindness
You do to her; and so dear Love farewel.
  El. Oh! stay! and do not make our farewel short,
For this is the last time I e're shall see thee.
  Gl. Do not say so, my Love.
  El. I know it is.
Thy Enemies are powerful, and many,
And thy own Innocence will betray thee to e'm.
  Gl. I hope not so, I doubt not but to scape
From all their Snares; and if I do, I'le come
And find thee out in thy poor barren Island,
There we'l be all the World to one another.
In that most desolate mournful abode
We will be happier, then e're we were
In the high stately building of our Greatness,
Whose walls were Vanity, foundations Rottenness.
Oh! I can speak no more to thee for Tears.
Once more farewel. ———*Exit.*
  El. All comfort go with thee,
For none abides with me, my Joy is death,
Death, at whose name I oft have been afraid,
Because I wish't this World's eternity;
But now I wish the World were at an end.
Stanly, I prethy go, and take me hence,
I care not whether, for I beg no favour.
I care not what becomes of wretched me,
My Honour is for ever sunk in shame,
And my Lord lost among his Enemies;
For I am sure they'l murder him amongst e'm,
And I shall never never see him more.
Prethee conveigh me where thou art commanded.
  Stan. Why, Madam, that is to the Isle of *Man,*
There to be us'd according to your State.
  El. According to my State? How's that? Reproachfully?
For now my State is vilest Infamy.
  Stan. Like to a Duchess, and Duke *Humphry*'s Lady,
According to that state you shall be us'd.
  El. Sheriff, farewel, I wish no harm to thee,
Though thou hast been conductor of my shame.
  Sher. It is my Office, Madam pardon me.
  El. I, I, farewel, thy Office is discharg'd.
Come, *Stanly,* let us go.
  Stan. Your Penance done;
Now, Madam, if you please, throw off your sheet.

El. My

El. My shame will not be thrown off with my sheet.
No, it will hang upon my richest Robes.
All Sin will meet dishonour, first or last,
I hope my Crown's to come, and my shame past.   *Exit.*

ACT IV.

Enter King, Queen, Cardinal, Suffolk, York, Buckingham.

King. I Admire my Lord of *Glocester* is not come,
'Tis not his wont to be the hindmost Man,
What e're occasion keeps him from us now.
   Queen. Do you not see his alter'd Countenance?
With what a Majesty he bears himself?
How proud, how peremptory, how unlike himself?
We know the time when he was mi'd and affable,
And if we did but glance a far-off look,
Immediately he was upon his Knee,
That all the Court admir'd his great humility.
But now he frowns, and passes stifly by,
Scorning to shew us any regard at all.
   Suff. Madam, most true, Has not the King observ'd
This carriage in him?
   Qu. He will see no ill in him.
Come, Sir, he is a Man exceeding dangerous,
He is no inconsiderable Person.
First, he is next the Crown, if you shou'd fall
He is the next that Mounts; that 'tis ill policy
To trust him with your Royal Person and Councels,
Whose rancorous mind is now prepar'd for mischief,
And whose advantage is the King's destruction,
Who else will gain by it? We shall be sad loosers;
But he will compass all his heart can wish,
Your Kingdoms, and revenge upon his Enemies.
   Card. The two great Idols of a proud mans heart.
   Suff. Oh! his Soul swell's with rancour as 'twere poyson'd,
He foams with Gall, and his Eyes flash with fury.
I saw him th' other day pass by the King,
And Queen, as they were walking in the Garden.
He measur'd oft the King from Head to Foot
With a disdainful eye, as who shou'd say,
Henry, Thou art too little for thy Throne,
Then wou'd he cast a down-look on the King,

And

The MURDER of the D. of GLOCESTER.

And press him with his eye to the Earth, and look on him
As if he lay under his Feet already,
Nay, under th' Earth; and then he stampt, and pointed
Towards *Paul's*, where his Wife lately did Penance,
As who shou'd say, Oh! *Henry*, very shortly
My Wife shall tread on thy cold Monument
With as much pride, as thou hast made her tread
With her bare feet, yon cutting Flints with shame.
In short, all his demeanour is of late
So raging, haughty, frantique and intolerable,
That I believe the Devil which his Wife
Conjur'd from Hell, is gotten into his Breast.

Card. He was a great frequenter of the Chappel,
No Man so constant, no Man so devout,
The lowest bower to the Altar there,
The highest lifter up of eyes to Heaven,
The humblest kneeler on the Marble Floor.
But now, as if he had gain'd all the Heaven,
He aim'd at by devotion, the Kingdom;
His Knees no more lick up the Chappel Dust
To blind the People's eyes, they are blind enough,
He takes no more the Chappel in his way,
He thinks he is at his journeys end, the Throne.

Qu. That's the next thing, Sir, makes him dangerous:
He has, by his Hypocrisie and Flattery,
So gull'd the credulous Commons of their hearts,
They'l venture Hanging at any time to Crown him,
And think it Martyrdom to die for him.

King. These things are very bad, if they be true.

Suff. True, Sir? His Wive's crime prove e'm; what do you think
Did instigate that *Bedlam* brainsick Woman
To her foul fault, but his foul subornation?
Or if he were not privy to her wickedness,
At least high vaunts of his Succession.
And letting fall some words to please her pride,
To shew what high designs he had near Birth,
Made the proud frantique Woman run immediately
To fetch a cursed Midwife out of Hell.

King. Indeed, that was a very wicked Fact.

Suff. Oh! Sir, the Duke of *Glocester* is a Man
Unsounded yet, and full of deep deceit.

Card. Sir, he appears to you to be a Man
Of great Humanity, Mildness, and Gentleness,
There's not a greater Tyrant upon Earth.
If any small Offences had at any time
Tript up the heels of any of his Enemies,

And

And thrown e'm in his power, he tortur'd e'm
Beyond all bounds either of Law or Manhood.
He has torn their Bodies so by horrid Deaths,
As if to put affronts upon that peaceful
Christianity which forbids all Revenge,
He'd put a cheat upon the Resurrection,
And tear that Article out of our Creed.
 King. Can this be true? How chance I never heard of it?
 Card. Who ever durst acquaint you this before?
 Suff. Who ever had your Ear but he till now?
 King. The meanest poorest Subject in my Kingdom
Had it, and shall, as much as he or any Man.
 Card. Ay! you like Heaven, Sir, gave access to all,
But he was that eternal Persecution,
All suffer'd that devoutly wou'd approach you.
 King. If this this be true, what a vile thing is Man?
 Yo. Sir, his insatiable Avarice
Makes two great Crowns sit loosely on your Head.
He squeez'd the *English* Purses till Blood followed,
Upon pretence to pay your Troops in *France*,
So almost tore this Kingdom from its Loyalty,
Then by not sending any of that Money;
He starv'd your Troops, and almost lost you *France*.
 Buck. Oh! there are horrid Crimes lie hid in smooth
Duke *Humphrey*, which the time will bring to light.
 King. My Lords, you seem to take great care of me
If it be real, it deserves great praise;
But shall I speak my Conscience freely to you?
No Man, I'me sure, no Monarch shou'd dissemble,
I do not, cannot think the Duke of *Glocester*
That horrid thing you represent him to me.
 Card. Then what are we, Sir?
 King. My Lord Cardinal,
I'le tell you what my Father said you were,
His Reason was as piercing as his Sword;
And he from depth of Knowledg, not from Prophesie,
Said, That if e're you were a Cardinal.
You'd make your Cap vye with your Prince's Crown.
As for these Lords, I wo'ld entreat of them
To think that I have Eyes as well as they.
If my Lord Duke of *Glocester* had such Sores
Break out of him as these, I shou'd ha' seen e'm
Some time or other, sure, as well as they.
If he had plaid such Proteus tricks as these,
Some time or other, sure, I shou'd have catch'd him.
But if he be the Monster they have painted him,

              Then

The MURDER of the D. of GLOCESTER.

Then what a horrid villanous thing is Man?
Who wou'd not rather live with Wolves than Men?
For a Wolf shews his nature, but a Man
Appears a Lamb, when he is most a Wolf.
If so, then I must fly from all of you;
For now when you seem Lambs, you may be Tygers.
 Qu. Sir, on my knees I humbly fall before you.   (*Kneels.*)
And beg with Tears, do not give up your self
And all of us to Death by incredulity.
I am a poor weak Woman, and a Stranger,
And of a Nation for whom your Subjects
By Nature, have an inbred scorn and hate,
Which great successes, greatly have improv'd.
And, Sir, my banish't Enemy the Duchess,
Will in the Rocks of her poor barren Island,
Sit brooding Vengeance, and when you are dead,
The Eagles she has hatcht shall tear my Soul out,
And who in *England* can or will protect me?
 Suff. And all of us are in the same condition.   *All kneel.*
 Qu. Then if you think these Lords, Sir, have no Loyalty,
Nor I the consort of your Youth no love,
Yet think we have some kindness for our selves,
And in your preservation seek our own.
 King. Rise my dear Love; rise all of you my Lords;
If I have injur'd you by my suspitions,
I pray forgive me, you perhaps have seen
More in the Duke of *Glocester*, than I have.
I must confess I'me of a temper fram'd
Wakeful to holy thinks, drowzy to earthly;
I'me as unfit for Earth, as some for Heaven.
Yet knowing I'me the Shepherd of my Flock,
I rouse my self to attend upon my Duty,
But oft I charm my self asleep again
With the Cælestial Musick of Religion,
And then a Wolf may steal upon my sleep
And I not see him, which perhaps you may.
That, Sirs, I thank you all for your kind care.
 Card. Sir, we have faithfully discharg'd our Consciences.
 King. You have done well, I thank you all; but pray
Give me good proofs of what you have alledged.
'Tis not enough to say, in such a Bush
There lies a Thief, in such a Cave a Beast,
But you must shew him to me e're I shoot,
Else I may kill one of my stragling Sheep,
I'me fond of no mans Person but his Vertue.
Prove that the Duke and Loyalty are strangers.

G   And

And he and I will be as far asunder
As Life and Death, the Grave shall be betwixt us.
 Suff. Oh! Sir, we shall not want sufficient proofs.

  Enter *the* Duke *of* Glocester, *they all start as soon as he comes in.*

 Card. See! see! the Duke is here.
 King. Ha! they all start
At the first sight of him, I like not that.——   (*Aside.*)
 Gl. All happiness attend my Lord the King.
Pardon, Royal Sir, that I have stayed so long.
 Suff. My Lord of *Glocester*, you are come too soon,
Unless you were more Loyal than you are.
My Lord, I here Arrest you of high Treason.
 Gl. My Lord of *Suffolk*, you shall not see me blush,
Nor change my Countenance at this Arrest.
 King. As they to see him did; he twits e'm well.—— (*Aside.*
 Gl. Innocence is not very easily daunted.
Who can accuse me? Wherein am I guilty?
 Yo. 'Tis thought, my Lord, that you took Bribes from *France*,
And being Protector, staid the Souldiers Pay,
By means whereof all *France* is almost lost.
 Gl. Is it but thought so? What are they that think so?
 King. Ha! Is it come but to a thought already?   (*Aside.*)
 Gl. I never rob'd the Souldiers of their Pay.
Nor ever had one penny Bribe from *France*.
But I have rob'd my self both day and night
Of all my rest, to study good for *England*.
The Farthing that e're I wrested from the King,
Or hoarded up for my own private use,
I wish may canker all, I can call mine;
But I have wrested from my own Revenues
Many a Pound, and given among the Garrisons,
Because I wou'd not Tax the needy Commons,
And never ask'd for Restitution.
 Card. It serves you well, my Lord, to say so much.
 Gl. I say no more than truth, so help me Heaven.
 Yo. In your Protectorship, you did invent
Strange and unheard of Tortures for Offenders,
That *England* was defam'd by Tyranny.
 Gl. It is well known, Pity was all my fault;
For I shou'd melt at an Offenders tears,
And humble words were Ransom oft for Faults.
I never gave condign Punishment,
Unless the Offender were a bloody Murtherer,
Or ravenous Thief, that fleec'd poor Passengers.

Suff.

The MURDER of the D. of GLOCESTER.

Suff. My Lord, these Faults are easie, quickly answer'd:
But mightier Crimes shall be laid to your Charge,
From which you cannot easily purge your self.
I then Arrest you in his Majestie's Name,
And here Commit you to my Lord Cardinal,
To keep you safely till your time of Trial.

King. So, they scarce know what to accuse him of   (*Aside.*)
And yet Arrest him, now I find e'm out.
My Lord of *Glocester*, 'tis my special hope,
That you will clear your self from all Suspition;
My Conscience tells me you are Innocent.

Gl. Ah! Gracious Prince, these Days are dangerous:
Vertue ne're saw good Times, but one wou'd think
If ever it shou'd find e'm 'twou'd be now,
Under the Reign of such a Saintlike King.
But now the Devil rages more than ever,
'Cause from the Angel-vertues of the King,
He almost fears the downfal of his Kingdom.
Under the Reigns of wicked Kings he sleeps,
Because he knows they do his Business for him;
But now he let's out all his fiercest Fiends,
And bids them do his worst, or all is lost.
Rancour, Ambition, and foul Subornation,
Are all at work to take away my Life,
The Devil will not be content without it.
If I by Death cou'd serve my King and Country,
I'de freelier give my Life, than these Lords take it.

King. My Lord, my Lord I do believe you.

Gl. Sir, I humbly thank you for your Royal Charity,
All these Lords know what you believe, my innocence.
Sad were my case, if there were proofs as strong
Of their foul Charge, as their foul Hate and rancour.
Their very looks are witnesses against e'm.
Beauford's red sparkling eyes tell his hearts malice,
And *Suffolk*'s cloudy brow his stormy hate.
Sharp *Buckingham* unburden's with his Tongue,
The envious load that lies upon his heart.
And dogged *York* that reaches at the Moon,
Because I have pluck'd back his roaming Arm,
Endeavours to pull Vengeance on my Head,
Nay, my Queen has with the rest conspir'd,
And with her best endeavour has stirr'd up
My Gracious King to be my Enemy:
Ay, all of you have laid your Heads together,
I had notice of your Plots and Conventicles,
And all to take away my guiltless Life.

G 2   I

I shall not want false Witness to condemn me,
Nor store of Treason to augment my Guilt.

Card. His railing, Sir, is most intolerable.
If those that watch to keep your Royal Person
From Treason's secret Knife, and Traytor's rage,
Be thus upbraided, chid, and rated at,
And the Offender granted scope of speech,
'Twill cool Men's zeal to serve your Majesty.

Suff. Has he not twit our Sovereign Lady here
With ignominious words, though subtilly couch't?
As if she had suborned Villains to swear
False Allegations, to destroy his Life?

Qu. But I can give the looser leave to rail.
Beshrew the Winners, for they play me false,
And well such Loosers may have leave to speak.

Buck. He'l wrest the sence, and hold us here all day.
Pray, my Lord Cardinal, look to your Prisoner.

Card. Sirs, take away the Duke, and guard him sure.

Gl. Ah! thus King *Henry* throws away his Crutch
Before his Legs be firm to bear his Body.
Farewel most gracious Sovereign, Heaven protect you,
You ne're stood more in need of his Protection,
For I'me afraid if Heaven does not save you,
Man will not; Oh! that all my fears were groundless.

King. Stay Uncle, let me embrace you e're I go!
I wish, (I speak it here before their faces)
I wish my Enemies had but thy innocence.
I in thy face behold, what I ne're saw,
Or in their looks, or any of their actions,
A map of Honour, Truth, and Loyalty.

Card. Oh! Sir! and do you thus——?——

King. Nay, Sirs, permit me,
You from my Bosom tear my best of Friends,
My wisest Councellor, my faithful'st Servant,
And the great torment forces me to speak.
Ah! yet, good Uncle, is the hour yet to come
That e're I found you false, or fear'd your Faith.
But there are louring Stars envy your state.
For these great Lords, and *Margaret* your Queen,
Do seek subversion of your harmless life,
And I your King want power to save you from e'm.

Gl. Ah, gracious Sovereign, send me quickly hence,
What ever innocence I had before,
I'me growing a great Criminal, my stay
Does make me guilty of your Royal Sorrows.

King. Thou need'st not beg to be sent hence, thy Enemies

Wil

The MURDER of the D. of GLOCESTER.

Will quickly send thee hence in spite of me.
   Gl. Oh! what a World is this, when such a King
Has little Power, because he has too much Goodness.
   Card. The Duke sure bears about him some Enchantment,
Wherewith he does bewitch the King! — Away with him.
   Gl. I will away; and from the World and you
Cou'd part, with greater joy than e're man left
A howling Desert full of Savage Beasts,
Did I not leave my Sovereign behind.
But, Oh! the joy of my escape is dash'd,
When I remember I have left him there
Bewildred, and no one to be his guid,
Begirt by Wolves, and none to be his guard.
   Card. What, are we Wolves? He does improve in railing.
   Gl. Prove your selves otherwise, I shall be glad;
Let all your wickedness end at my death,
And I'le forgive you that with all my heart.
I will thank Heaven for my destiny,
If as the Roman *Curtius*, stop'd the Plague
By leaping down into the gaping Earth;
So I by being thrown into the Grave,
Cou'd stop the plague of your Ambition.
But I'me afraid I shall do no such miracle.
   Suff. This is intolerable! My Lord Cardinal,
Why do you stand so tamely, and permit him
To wound both yours, and all our Honours thus?
   Card. I will endure no more, away with him.
   King. Farewel, good Man.
   Gl. Farewel, oh! best of Kings.   (*Exit with a Guard.*)
   King. So the inhumane Souldier from the panting
Breasts of his trembling Mother tears an Infant,
And carries it away before her face
Upon his bloody Spear; whilst she looks on
And swoons, and falls, and dares not call for help.
Even so remorseless ha' they born him hence,
Whilst I with as unhelpless tears bewail
The good Man's injuries, and with dim'd eyes
Look after him, and cannot do him good,
So mighty are his vowed Enemies;
Whom he I'me sure ne're wrong'd, he ne're wrong'd any Man.   *Exit.*
   Qu. Do you see, my Lords, in what a case we are?
The King will hear nothing against the Duke.
The King is cold, full of foolish pity,
And *Glocester*'s shew beguiles his easie mind,
Just as a Snake roul'd in a flowry Bank,
Which shining checker'd slough does sting a Child,

That

That for the beauty thinks it excellent.
Believe me, Lords, were none more wife than I,
And I believe my felf not dull in this,
This *Glocefter* fhou'd be quickly rid of the World,
To free the King from danger, us from fear.

 Card. That he fhou'd die, is worthy Policy;
But yet we want fome Colour for his death,
And it is meet he die by courfe of Law.

 Suff. That were a worthy policy indeed,
To bring him to the Bar, and there for want
Of good fubftantial Arguments againft him,
Shall openly arreign our felves of Malice;
And fo inftead of bringing him to death,
Expofe our felves to all the People's fury.
True, we have Jealoufie back'd with ftrong Reafons,
But Reafon cannot enter into their minds;
Mud Walls, you know, refift all Battery.
And then from thofe Mud Walls, the People's fury
Will falley out, and make flaughter on us.

 Yo. I'me o' your mind, it is diftraction
To fail with him into his own fafe Harbour
The People's rage, and not be well coyl'd round
With proofs, that will refift fmall fhot at leaft.

 Qu. What fhall we do then? Muft we let him live?
If fo, let's find fome way our felves to die;
For I had rather perifh once for all,
Than die each hour a lingring death of fear.

 Suff. No, Madam, no, the imperious Duke fhall die,
We will not to his pride and rage expofe
The King, the Kingdom, and our felves, and do
Subftantial wrong to all, becaufe we cannot
Do againft him a formal piece of Juftice.
Muft Juftice ftarve, becaufe we want a Lawyers
Forked diftinctions to feed her neatly with;
And bright keen proofs to carve him up withal?
No, let us examine into her hungry Stomach
The morfel any way, no matter how.
Nor will the Duke have any injury,
It is an honeft, and a good deceit
To deceive him who firft intends deceit.

 Qu. Moft gallant *Suffolk*, refolutely fpoke.

 Suff. Not refolute except fo much were done,
For things are often fpoke, and never meant.
To fhew my Heart and Tongue fully agree,
Say but the word, I'le be the Executioner;
And think I do a meritorious deed.

The MURDER of the D. of GLOCESTER.

I know the Duke means Treason to the King,
Why shou'd I stay for proofs of what I know?
Does any one refuse to kill a Wolf,
Till he has stain'd his Chops, with Crimson Blood?
No, 'tis enough he knows him for a Wolf,
His nature's Crime enough to deserve death.
He then does best, that does dispatch him soonest.
What do you say Lord Cardinal? Speak your mind,
You see how free we are, why are you close?
Is it a meritorious deed, or no?

   Card. My Lords, I only staid to feel your Pulses.
That I might know the temper of your minds,
How vigorous their constitutions were.
Religion has a body and a spirit,
The body is like Water, weak and tasteless,
And that we fling among the Common People;
The extracted Spirit is intoxicating,
And that we drink our selves, and give our Friends.
And as wise Men do always in their pleasures
Select Companions of their own Humour,
Those that are rude and quarrelsome in Drink,
They shun with care; those that are kind and pleasant,
Witty and good natur'd, gladly they Consort withal,
So we ne're drink the spirit of Religion,
With any Men but those of our own minds,
Or Men of melting maudling piety,
Who when they are drunk with it, will kiss our feet,
And weep, and do whatever we command e'm.

   Suff. And pray, what is this Spirit? let us taste it.

   Card. This! Did some ask me if this deed were lawful,
I wou'd say no, it is a horrid Murder.
If any Man offend's against the Publick,
He to the Publick must give satisfaction;
That private Man that kil's him is a Murderer,
And a bold Robber of the publick Right.
But now to you I say, cut the Duke's Throat,
'Tis lawful, necessary, meritorious.
And so 'twere in another, but perhaps
If I shou'd say so he wou'd not believe it,
So he might wound the Church with its own Weapons:
I'd pronounce all such damn'd, shou'd kill the Duke,
But I'le pronounce you damn'd if you refuse it,
Because you are capable of these great mysteries.

   Suff. Most excellent! this deed which I before
Only thought needful, now I find Religious.

   Card. A most religious, meritorious deed.

                                                      You

You know the Churches Power is call'd the Keys,
The Keys are given us, not one single Key,
As if there were only one Door to Heaven.
Oh! there are many entrances! There's one
Great common Gate of common Honesty,
At that we let in common understandings;
Then there are private Wickets, but the Stairs
That lead up to e'm, are most steep and dangerous,
And none dare venture up but bold brave Spirits;
But these back Stairs lead up to Heaven's best Rooms.
This Murder then is one of Heaven's back Stairs.
Kill him, his Blood will oyl the Churches Keys,
That you shall choose what Room in Heaven you please.
   Yo. I ne're heard any thing that pleas'd me better.
   Card. My Lords, my Lords, Reason and Law allow
You Layicks to carry Swords for your defence,
Religion suffers us to carry none.
Is it because Priests Altars and Religion
Does not deserve defence as well as you?
Yes, but we Priests have always Weapons ready,
A kind of two-edge Knives, call'd Subtilties,
That are most keenly whetted at the Altars,
And nothing cuts so as one of them.
In short then, kill the Duke, kill him to night,
Before he hurt the King, the Church, or you.
   Suff. Here is my hand, my Lord, I'le see it done.
   Qu. I give consent.
   Yo. I'le joyn; and now we four
Agree in it, who dares oppose a Censure?
   Suff. We must get fitting People to assist us.
   Card. I'le find you such, I'le mould e'm for the purpose.
When we have kill'd the Duke, we will give out
He kill'd himself to prevent publick shame,
Or his heart broke because he was discovered.
   Suff. But will not those be Lyes?
   Card. Most sacred truths.
Do not his actions bring his death upon him?
   Qu. True.
   Card. Then 'tis true, I hope he kills himself.
   Suff. Right.
   Card. Or suppose we report the discovery
Of his foul treacherous actions broke his heart:
I pray, is that false, when the discovery
Of his foul actions make us break his Neck?
   Suff. No, certainly, for that will break his heart.

Card.

The MURDER of the D. of GLOCESTER.

Card. Then every way you see, we spread no falshoods.
My Lords, the Church has several kind of Garments,
Course home-spun Clothes for Fools, fine Robes for Wits.
Now though a Fool may be let into Heaven
With his course Coat on, they will ne're admit him
To Rooms of State, among the Saints of quality.

Enter a Gentleman.

Gent. My Lords, I am sent Post to you from *Ireland*.
The Irish Rebels are all up in Arms,
And put the English to the Sword, send Succours
With all the speed you can, and stop the rage
Betimes, or else the Wound may grow incurable.
Card. A Breach that craves a very speedy stop.
What counsel give you in this weighty Business?
Suff. That speedy Force be rais'd. My Lord of *York*,
Pray do you Head e'm, and go try your Fortune.
Yo. I will, my Lord, so please his Majesty.
Suff. Why, our Authority is his consent,
And what we do establish he confirms.
Then pray, my Lord, take you this task in hand.
Yo. Content, my Lords, do you provide me Souldiers,
Whilst I take orders for my own Affairs.
Suff. To raise you men, my Lord, shall be my business.
And now return we to the false Duke *Humphry*.
Card. Let us about the work immediately.
Things of great weight must not be carried long
For fear we shou'd tire under e'm; and now
The gaudy blabbing, and remorseful day
Is crept into the bosom of the Sea,
And in the room more fitting for our purpose,
The silent pitiless stern-night is risen,
And beckens us methinks with her black hand;
To do that gallant work under her Wings,
Will make her fam'd in the Records of Time,
Who else will like a drop fall in the Sea
Of black Oblivion, and be lost for ever.
Suff. Come then, I flame with fury to be at it,
That I shall need no Flambeau but my self.
Card. We two, my Lord, will be the chief performers,
But yet we must have some trusty assistants,
And I will go and fashion some immediately;
I always have store of soft Clay prepar'd,
Which I can mould into what shape I please.

H *Suff.*

Suff. Madam, please you to go to your Repose,
And dream of Crowns and Scepters, the high Wall
That kept you from e'm, shall fall down to Night,
And your way open'd to the Royal Seat.

Qu. And thou shalt happy be when I am great. (*Aside to him.*

Yo. So Lords, I thank you, you have done my business, (*Ex. S. Q. C.*
I wanted men and you will give e'm me;
I wanted *Glocester*'s death, you give me that too.
Now lies the King as open to destruction,
As a poor Ship tost on the open Sea,
With Masts all broken, and the Sailers mad.
I have seduc'd one *Cado*, a headstrong Kentishman,
To take on him the name of *Mortimer*,
And make Commotion. I have seen in *Ireland*
That Fellow fight, till his thighs full of Darts,
Were almost like two sharp-quill'd Porcupines.
Then have I seen him dance like a *Morisco*,
Shaking the bloody Darts, as he his Bells.
In Face, and Gate, and Speech, he's like dead *Mortimer*.
Thus shall I try how men affect our Title.
If he be ta'ne and Rack'd, he'l ne're confess.
And if he thrives, I'le reap the Rascal's harvest.
Then pious *Henry* to a Covent gone,
And *Humphry* to his Tomb, I'le climb the Throne. (*Exit.*

Enter the Cardinal, Suffolk, *and three* Murderers.

Suff. Are you provided, my Lord Cardinal?
Card. Of three brave Fellows.
Suff. What? old hardned Villains?
Card. Of better instruments, of soft Church Tools
Which I have heated with the fire of Zeal,
And I can bow e'm any way I please.
These are the honest men! —— Come honest men!
You are design'd to be most glorious men;
Glorious on Earth, and glorious in Heaven.

Suff. I will provide for e'm on Earth, my Lord,
The other place do you look after, for e'm.

Card. How? I provide for e'm in Heaven, my Lord?
They'l have more share in Heaven than my self.

1. *Mur.* Oh! my good Lord!
Card. Nay, it is true, my Friends.
Suff. My Lord, you will instruct e'm what to do.
Card. I have instructed, and encourag'd e'm,
Told e'm their business, and the nature of it,
That 'tis a charity to the whole Church.

I've

The MURDER of the D. of GLOCESTER. 51

I've told e'm, stopping of a Heretick's Windpipe,
Is stopping a wide Leak sprung in the Church,
Where streams of Heresie flow in to drown it;
Which if they will not stop, especially
When I a Pilot in the Church command e'm,
They will not only cast away their own
Poor ruin'd Souls, but many thousands more.

  Suff. Sure, nothing is more plain.

  1. *Mur.* Nothing, my Lord.

  2. *Mur.* Oh! may it please your Grace, 'tis very plain.

  3. *Mur.* Pshaw! pshaw! 'tis not so plain, and I do'nt like it.
'Tis not so plain, I'me sure, as I want Money.   *(Aside.*

  Card. Well, I need say no more, I'le only give e'm
An Oath of secrecy; come to me presently
About that Business.

  1. *Mur.* ⎱
           We'l attend your Grace.   *(Ex. Card. Suff.*
  2. *Mur.* ⎰

  3. *Mur.* I don't know what to think o' this damn'd business.

  1. *Mur.* What shou'd you think! 'Tis stopping of a Leak.

  3. *Mur.* Do not talk to me of stopping of a Leak!
It is a cursed Murder.

  2. *Mur.* How, a Murder!
The Cardinal said it is a work of charity.

  3. *Mur.* It is so, to my starving Wife and Children,
I shall stop Leaks in their poor empty Bellies,
And that's the thing that satisfies my Conscience.

  1. *Mur.* That's not enough, you may get Money otherwise.

  3. *Mur.* I cannot, I take pains, and pray, and fast,
And am so fearful to displease a Saint,
That I keep every day a Holy-day,
And yet I cannot thrive.

  2. *Mur.* That's very strange.

  3. *Mur.* I got a little Money the other day,
And went, and gave half of it to a Priest,
To pray for me, and give me a little counsel,
What course I had best take to get some Money.
He gave me a heavenly Prayer, and bid me say it
For thirty days together, and after that
He said I shou'd obtain what e're I ask'd for.
I did, and at the end of thirty days,
I pray'd to Heaven to give me thirty pounds;
Then I watch'd night and day, almost a Week,
To see if any thing wou'd bring the Money;
The devil of any one brought me a farthing.

  1. *Mur.* That's very strange.

  3. *Mur.* I went and told the Priest

H 2   What

What luck I had; he bad me go to *Canterbury*,
And pray devoutly to St. *Thomas Becket*.
I went and pray'd to St. *Thomas*, and St. *Thomas*,
But might as well have pray'd to St. *Tom Thumb*,
For any thing I got.

 2. *Mur.* That's very strange.

 3. *Mur.* I went again, and told the Priest my luck,
And then he gave me a miraculous Prayer,
Said, if that wou'd not do, then nothing wou'd.
He said, the other day in *Germany*,
A high dutch Lady had her Head cut off,
And yet liv'd after it, two and twenty hours.

 2. *Mur.* After her Head was off?

 3. *Mur.* After 'twas off.

 1. *Mur.* Good-lack, is't possible?

 3. *Mur.* She cou'd not die
Till she Confest, and had Communicated,
And then her Head and Body agreed to die,
And in her Grave it seems this prayer was found.

 2. *Mur.* And did you say it?

 3. *Mur.* Ay, forty times a day,
For forty days.

 1. *Mur.* And was you e're the richer?

 3. *Mur.* The devil a farthing.

 2. *Mur.* Oh! Good-lack! good-lack!

 3. *Mur.* On this I went and told the Cardinal all.

 1. *Mur.* And what said he to you?

 3. *Mur.* He made me kneel,
And thank St. *Thomas*, and the high dutch Lady,
For they had heard my Prayers, and sent me to him,
To do a work wou'd gain me Heaven and Earth.

 2. *Mur.* Why look you there now!

 1. *Mur.* Look you, look you there now.

 3. *Mur.* But that same work, was this same scurvy business.

 2. *Mur.* A scurvy business? Do you call a blessing
Sent from St. *Thomas*, and the high dutch Lady,
A scurvy business?

 3. *Mur.* Why shou'd I believe
It came from them? for both their Throats were cut;
Why shou'd I think that they love cutting Throats?
They cou'd not find it such a pleasant business.

 1. *Mur.* They love to cut the throat of a vile Heretick.

 3. *Mur.* How do I know Duke *Humphry* is a Heretick?

 2. *Mur.* The Cardinal says he is one.

 3. *Mur.* How if the Cardinal
Shou'd be mistaken?

The MURDER of the D. of GLOCESTER.

1. *Mur.* He will answer for it.
3. *Mur.* And so he shall, for I'me an honest Fellow,
And if to kill Duke *Humphry* be a sin,
I'le either lay it at the Cardinal's door,
Or put it on the high dutch Lady's score. —— *Ex. Mur.*

Enter Cardinal and three Murderers.

Card. So, you have all sworn at the holy Altars;
Now have a care, don't let your Consciences
Fool you, to flinch with fear e're it is done,
Or to repent and tell it when 'tis done;
If so you are trebly Damn'd.
  1. *Mur.* I warrant your Grace.
  Card. Believe your Priests, and not your Consciences,
For Priests are to direct your Consciences;
Your Consciences are silly, false, corrupt.
  2 *Mur.* Oh! hang my Conscience, Sir, I ne're regarded it.
  3 *Mur.* May I be bold to ask your Grace one question?
  Card. Ay, prethee do.
  3 *Mur.* Suppose a Priest, an't please you,
Mistake, and I shou'd sin by his command,
Will he be damn'd for me? and shall I escape?
  Card. A Priest mistake? Sirrah, were you ne're catechis'd,
That you are ignorant of First Principles?
  1 *Mur.* Why, look you now, you will be asking questions.
  Card. The Church cannot mistake, the Church is infallible.
  3 *Mur.* Pray Sir, an't please you, how shall I know that?
  Card. How shall you know it, Sirrah? The Church tells you so.
  2 *Mur.* Prethee give over, don't stand asking questions.
  3 *Mur.* How shall I know the Church tells true, an't please you?
  Card. The Church, I say, Sirrah, is Infallible.
  3 *Mur.* How shall I know the Church is so Infallible?
  Card. Why I say, Sirrah, the Church tells you so.
  3 *Mur.* But how shall I be certain it tells true?
  1 *Mur.* What a strange man is this? we must dismiss him?
  Car. Be certain, this is a damn'd Rogue! —— a Heretick!
Sirrah, don't you believe the Church? I'le burn you.
  2 *Mur.* So, so, you have brought your self into a fine pickle.
  3 *Mur.* Oh! yes, Sir, I believe!
  1 *Mur.* Oh! do you so.
  2 *Mur.* 'Tis time you shou'd.
  3 *Mur.* I only did make bold to ask some questions,
To know some things, that I was ignorant of
  Card. Why there was your mistake, you are not to know,
You are only to do what a Priest bids you;

Priests

Priests only are to know, you are to know nothing
Except your duty, and the reward that follows it.
Your duty now is to destroy a Traytor,
Yes, and a Heretick.

   3 *Mur.* I'le do't, an't please you.

   1 *Mur.* Your Grace may trust him, he is an honest Fellow,
Only a little troublesome with scruples.

   2 *Mur.* Which way, Sir, had we best to kill the Duke?

   Card. Which way it shall please Heaven to inspire you.
Stay, let me see! ——Strangling I think were best.
Ay strangling! strangling! 'twill give least suspition,
And make the World believe, Grief broke his heart;
For so we will give out.

   1 *Mur.* We'l do't an't please you.
I have a Handkerchief fit for the purpose.

   Card. Open the door, go to him, go, go, quickly.
        The Scene is drawn, the Duke of Gloccster sitting and
            reading in his Night-Gown.

   Card. Ha! he's awake, and up; you two go hold him   (*Softly to*
And get him down, whilst the other strangles him.   *the Mur.*

   Gl. Ha! Who is that opens the door?

   2 *Mur.* The Cardinal's
Servants, an't please your Grace.

   Gl. And what's your business?

   1 *Mur.* The Cardinal saw your Light burning so late,
And was afraid your Grace was indispos'd;
And sent to know if your Grace wanted any thing,
And gave us strict command to wait upon you.

   Gl. He is grown wondrous kind; I am afraid
He's ill, for this is not his natural temper.
He guesses right of me, I'm ill indeed;
A heaviness like Death oppresses me.
I cannot get my thoughts out of a Grave:
I fear not Death it self, why shou'd a dream
And empty shadow of it then oppress me?

   Card. So, get behind him now whilst he is musing.   (*Aside.*

   Gl. If wicked men be digging now my Grave,
And these cold Terrors be fore-running damps,
Oh! Heaven prepare me for it.   (*Aside.*

   3 *Mur.* How he prays!   (*Aside.*
   2 *Mur.* What if he does? What are a Hereticks prayers?   (*Aside.*
   Gl. Let all my sins drop from me in these Tears.
   3 *Mur.* How penitent he is! ——my Soul relents,
The Devil take this cursed want of Money.   (*Aside.*

   Gl. If e're my Person, Greatness, or Authority,

                                                         Did

The MURDER of the D. of GLOCESTER.

Did injure any one, forgive the fault,
And in the bosome of the injur'd person,
Pour down a thousand blessings. ——Above all things
Preserve the King from all his Enemies.
If I by Wickedness and Falshood perish,
Oh! give my bloody Enemies repentance,
And let my Death be an occasion
Of good to them, but ruine to their wickedness.

 3 *Mur.* Heark, how he prays for us that are his murderers!   (*Aside*
 1 *Mur.* What if he does? he is a Heretick.
His Prayers are Curses, we are the worse for e'm.   (*Aside.*
 Card. Why don't you do your work?   (*Aside.*
 3 *Mur.* We will, we will.   (*Aside.*
 Gl. So shall I do more good in Death than Life,
And by my innocent Death procure a Blessing
To my good King, my Country, all my Enemies.
    They lay hold on the Duke and strangle him.

 Card. So! Is he dead yet?
 2 *Mur.* Yes! he does not stir.

    Enter the Duke of Suffolk.

 Suff. Ho! What's the News?
 Card. The deed is done, my Lord.
 Suff. Have you dispatch'd the thing?
 1 *Mur.* We have done his business.
 Suff. Thou art a gallant Rogue! there's Gold for thee.
And for you all.
 Card. A Rogue, my Lord, you wrong him;
He is a Saint, and so are they all.
 3 *Mur.* A Saint: (*Aside.*
Devil take such Saints.
I wou'd this deed were to be done again,
My Family shou'd starve e're I wou'd do it.
 Card. I hear a noise without.
 3 *Mur.* A noise without!
I'me sure I hear a cursed noise within me,
A bawling Conscience.
 Card. Place the Body some way
As may give least suspition, and be gone,
And come another time for your rewards.
   They place the Body in a Chair, shut the Scene,—— and Ex.

                 Enter

Enter the King *and* Queen, Attendants.

Qu. What brings your Majesty abroad so early?
You do not use to finish your Devotion
So soon as this.
  King. Oh! Love, I am not well,
My Uncle is always walking in my mind,
And shakes the melancholy Room with fear;
Methinks he tells me I have not done well,
To give him up to his too cruel Enemies,
To men who are not such as they shou'd be.
  Qu. Why, Sir, have you so great mistrust of e'm?
  King. I wish I had no cause; I've sent Commands to e'm,
To bring my Uncle to me presently.

Enter the Cardinal.

Had you my message, my Lord Cardinal?
  Card. Yes, Royal Sir, the Duke of *Suffolk* instantly
Will bring the Duke of *Glocester*; I have lodg'd
My noble Prisoner but in the next Rooms.
  King. Methinks he shou'd not be the man you make him.
  Card. Your Majesty has your eyes always fixt
On shining Heaven, that when you look below,
The World is in a mist and dark to you.

Enter Suffolk.

  King. How now? Why look'st thou pale? why do'st thou shake?
Where is my Uncle? What's the matter? Speak.
  Suff. The Duke is dead.
  Card. How! Dead?
  Suff. Dead in his Chair.
  Qu. Oh! Heaven forbid!
  Suff. 'Tis true.
  Card. Heaven's secret Judgments.
I fear'd some dreadful judgment wou'd o'retake him.
The King Swoons.

  Qu. How is my Lord? Help, help, the King is dying.
  Suff. Rear up his Body, fetch some Water quickly.
  Qu. Oh! Help, help, help.
  Suff. See, he revives again.
Madam, be comforted.
  Qu. How does my Lord?

King.

The MURDER of the D. of GLOCESTER.

King. Oh! heavenly God! ——*Sighs deeply.*
Suff. Take comfort, Gracious Sir.
King. Ah! Wo is me for *Glocester!* wretched man!
Qu. Is all your comfort shut up in his Tomb?
And can you find no joy in me at all?
Why do you turn away and hide your Face?
I am no loathsome Leaper, look on me.
Ah! wo is me, more wretched than he is.
Did I for this expose my self to Winds,
And Rocks, and Seas, and twice was almost wrack'd,
And twice was driven back, as if the Winds
Forewarn'd me landing on this unkind Shore!
The vaulting Sea danc'd with me to and fro,
As it were loth to bring me to this Coast.
The Rocks cover'd in the Waves, and hid themselves,
As shaming to owe kindred to an Island,
Whose cruel King wou'd thus reward my Love.
Ah! see if he will speak to me, or look on me!
How hateful am I grown! Ah! wretched me!
Card. I see the King loves this dead Traytor better
Than all his living Friends! Farewel,—— I'me sorry Sir,
To see you hate your Friends, and love your Enemies. (*Ex.*
King. Where is my dead Friend? I'le see him—— lead me to him.
Suff. In the next Room, Sir: Ho, open these doors.

The Scene is drawn, and the Duke of Glocester *is shewn dead in a Chair.*

King. Oh! thou good man! And hast thou thus been us'd?
And is this all of thee that's left to me?
Oh! to how little, and how poor a pittance
Are all my Comforts in this life now brought!

Enter Warwick.

War. Oh! Sir, Reports are spread among the People,
The good Duke *Humphry* treacherously is murder'd,
By *Suffolk*'s and the Cardinal *Beauford*'s means.
Suff. By mine?
War. By yours.
Suff. I did expect as much.
War. The Commons, like a Hive of angry Bees,
That want their Leader, scatter up and down,
And care not whom they sting in their revenge.
I have endeavour'd to allay their rage,
Until they are satisfied about his death.
King. Ah! my Lord he is dead, 'tis true! too true!

I   See

See here: —But how he died, God knows, not I.
I fear foul play was plaid him for his Life.
Oh Heaven! to whom Judgment alone belongs,
Forgive me if I injure any one
With false suspitions.

War. Sir, as certainly,
As I believe that Heaven was his Maker,
I believe Treachery was his destroyer.

Suff. Do you know it, that so dreadfully you swear it?

War. I swear that I believe it.

Suff. What's your reason?

War. I see already above a thousand proofs,
That he was basely strangled.

Suff. Strangled!

War. Strangled.
His Face is black and swell'd with settled Blood,
Which shews the passage to the Heart was stopt,
Whether the Blood in natural deaths descends,
To aid the labouring Heart in his last conflict;
And failing, freezes with the cold of Death,
And ne're returns, but leaves the face all pale.
His eyes stand gastly from his Head, and almost
Come out to meet us to complain of strangling.
His gaping nostrils are stretch'd out with striving,
His hands are spread abroad, as one that grasp'd
And tugg'd for Life, but was by strength o're-master'd.
His well proportion'd Beard, is rugged made
Like Summer's Corn, by furious tempest lodg'd.
See a blew Ring encompasses his Neck.
Oh! Murder here has danc'd her fairy round.
If the Duke was not strangled, ne're was man.

Suff. Why, who shou'd do it, my Lord? none but my self
And Cardinal *Beauford*, had him in protection.

War. Who finds the Heifer dead, and bleeding fresh,
And sees a Butcher with his Ax stand by,
May easily suspect who made the Slaughter.

Qu. The Cardinal, and you, my Lord, are Murderers!
For shame, my Lord of *Warwick*, rule your arrogance.

War. Pray, Madam, let me with due reverence tell you,
Each word you speak for him, slaunders your Honour.

Suff. Blunt-witted Lord, thy evil manners say,
Thy Mother took into her blameful Bed
Some rough untutour'd Churl; and grafted there
On *Nevil's* noble race a rugged Clown.

War. Did not my Sovereign's presence check my fury,
I'de make thee kneel for pardon for this speech,

And

The MURDER of the D. of GLOCESTER.

And say, 'twas thy own Mother that thou mean'st,
And after this low homage, I wou'd kill thee,
Thou treacherous murderer of sleeping men.
  Suff. Thou shalt be waking when I shed thy blood;
If er'e I meet thee from this royal presence.
  War. Away, or I will drag thee! —— though I scorn thee,
I'le fight with thee, to appease Duke *Humphry*'s Ghost.
  King. Forbear my Lords, for shame! stay, I command you.

A Noise, Enter Salisbury.

  Sal. Great Sir, the Commons humbly implore by me,
The Duke of *Suffolk* may be put to death,
Or Banish'd instantly; for else they threaten,
They'l tear him hence by violence and Torture him.
Free from bold contradiction to your liking,
But out of Loyalty they drive him from you.
They say, If you desir'd to sleep, and charg'd
No one on pain of Death shou'd dare to wake you;
Yet if they saw a Serpent in your Bosom,
They with the hazard of their lives wou'd wake you,
And drive him from you whether you wou'd or no.
They say the Duke of *Suffolk* is that Serpent,
By whose envenom'd sting your Uncle perish'd;
A Prince a thousand times of *Suffolk*'s value,
From him they also fear your Majestie's Death.
  Suff. They durst not send this message to their King,
My noble Lord Embassador from *Weavers*.
  King. My Lord of *Salisbury*, Tell e'm from me,
I thank e'm for their Loyal care of me;
That I have been awake long e're they rouz'd me,
And seen the dangerous Serpent I have cherish'd
To my great danger, and my Friends destruction.
For oh! the slimy paths the Serpent crawl'd
To sting my Friend to Death, shine in my eyes.
  Suff. Sir, will you judg me e're you know my innocence?
  King. Go tell e'm, By that Heavenly Majesty,
Whose most unworthy Deputy I am,
I vow most solemnly, the English Air
Shall not receive three days infection more
From this most wicked man; for if it does
The fourth shall end his wickedness and him.   *Exit Salis.*
  Suff. Sir, this is hard to doom me e're I'me tried.
  Qu. Oh! let me plead, Sir, for this injur'd Lord.
  King. Oh fye, forbear! forbear! your pleading for him
Will add but very little to your Honour,

But to my anger much; 'twill make me pass
Censure on you, and heavier Doom on him.
Had I but said it, nothing shou'd ha chang'd me;
But having sworn it, you may easier
Remove the Kingdom than stay that man in it.
Then let him hear his Sentence once again:
If after three days space he shall be found
On any Ground that I am Ruler of,
The World shall not be Ransom for his Life. *Exit.*

Qu. Oh wretched! wretched me! Oh! I cou'd turn
My Breath and Spirits all, all into Curses,
Curse all thy Enemies, and all the World.
I prethee joyn with me, and let us Curse e'm.

Suff. A Plague upon e'm! Wherefore shou'd I curse e'm?
Were Curses killing as the groans of Mandrakes.
I'de stay to curse e'm were the Palace burning,
And every word I said were half on't fire,
And I, my Curses ended, shou'd be Ashes.
For what's the difference 'tween being Ashes,
Or Water, as I soon shall be with Sorrow?

Qu. I must betake my self now to my Tears,
The last poor refuge of a wretched Woman.

Suff. Must I see this? And can I not revenge it?
Like one of the fallen Spirits banish'd Heaven.
I stand upon the shining Precipice,
And look with grief on all the Joys I'me leaving;
Then down with Terror on my desperate fall,
Then grin with rage because I cannot help my self;
And amidst all these Passions, I'me more tortur'd
In Heaven, than I shall be when fallen to Hell.

Qu. My griefs no flesh can bear, no soul can guess.
Oh! that the moment when thou took'st me Prisoner,
Thy Sword had seperated my Soul and Body,
Then had I been at ease; but now thy Banishment
Divides e'm, and I live to feel the torment.

Suff. I'le stay with you, what ever shall befal me.

Qu. What shou'd befal but Death to both of us?
The strong convulsions of my griefs have tir'd,
Wasted, and weakned so my vanquish't Spirits,
That I am fainting now into a calm.

Suff. And in this calm the current of my Sorrows,
Shall bear my drowning Spirits to thy Bosom,
And lay it there as on a Bank of Lillies,
Where I will Die as in a pleasing slumber.

Qu. This must not be, we must not stay together,
No we must part, or staying thou must Die.

The MURDER of the D. of GLOCESTER.

I rather will endure a lingring Death
Of a long parting, than by Death to lose thee.
Whilst we are living we may meet again.
   Suff. We may, we shall, the King is not Immortal,
Or if he were, his Anger is not so.
But both will have an end, so will our Sorrows.
The longest life has still an utmost point:
No Creature is infinite.
   Qu. Except my Love.
   Suff. In hopes then once to meet again,—— Farewel!
   Qu. Oh! sad heart-breaking word! ——Where e're thou wandrest
Send to me oft.
   Suff. What joy shall I have else?
All Places will be desolate, and I
Shall live no longer than I hear you live.
   Qu. My Fit returns again! unhappy we!
Why are we two so nearly joyn'd in Love,
And yet by Fortune kept so wide asunder,
First by thy Marriage, and now by thy Banishment?
My Love was thrown as soon as it was Born
On cold Dispair, hearing thou hadst a Wife.
Hadst thou had none, and only been a Shepherd,
And known no other wealth than a small Flock,
No other Title than the charming Swain,
(For so wou'd every Shepherdess have call'd thee)
I wou'd have rather been thy humble Wife,
Than Queen to *Henry.*
   Suff. If I shou'd stay here
Till I told o're the Wealth I wou'd have given,
For such a happiness, we ne're shou'd part.
   Qu. Oh! must we part! Heaven made us for each other,
And then did set us two, of all the World,
Farthest asunder; a Wife first did part us,
But now whole Kingdoms, and whole Worlds must part us.
These Miseries I might have well expected;
My Love was born under Captivity,
I was thy Prisoner, e're my heart was so:
Chains lay at th' entrance of the gate of Love,
And pail Dispair forbad me entring in;
Yet such sweet Prospects drew my heart along,
It entred in, and now is lost for ever.
   Suff. Say not for ever; Do not cruelly
Put out the eyes of our Prophetick hopes,
Which like so many Angel-guides, will lead
Our Souls to pleasant Prospects of delight,
Where we may gaze till Fate is tir'd with frowning,

And

And Time with holding two so bent to meet,
Shall loose his hold, and let us flie together.
Till then farewel.
   Qu. Take with thee my poor heart.
   Suff. A Jewel lock'd into the wofull'st Cabinet
That ever did contain so great a Treasure.
Just like a splitted Bark, so sunder we.
This way sink I to ruine.
   Qu. This way I.——   *Exeunt several ways.*

The SCENE the Cardinals Apartment.

Enter the Cardinal.

   Card. I'me vext! I'me more, I'me wrack'd! By what? who knows?
By a thing within me call'd a Conscience.
A Trick,—— a Spring, that catches us, and pinches,
If we but point at an ill Action.
Why is it an ill thing to kill a man?
He is the Plague and Sickness of the World.
'Tis a kind honest thing to kill a man,
You cure the World of one Disease, you free
Thousands from Mischief, and you ease the man.
Yet if one do a man so great a kindness,
The damn'd ungrateful Rogue torments one's Conscience.
Men are ungrateful Rogues, living or dead.
I know not what to do; I must have ease.
Ho there!

Enter a Servant.

   Ser. My Lord.
   Card. Call my Physitian.
Stay there!—— What shou'd I do with a Physitian?
No Physick can give me any ease, but Poyson.
The gravel of the Grave is the best scowring
For such fierce Hawks as I am, after feeding.
Go, now I think on't, call my Confessor.
Let him alone!—— What shou'd I do with him too?
My Soul is sick, and it can have no ease,
I grow sick.——
Unless it purge (forsooth) in a Priest's ear.
Fetch me a Glass of Wine, run quickly,—— run.
I tremble!—— a cold sweat comes over me,
All the Air tastes of an infernal damp.

The

The MURDER of the D. of GLOCESTER. 63

The Ghost of Duke Humphry appears and goes out, the Cardinal falls into a Swoon. Enter the Servant with Wine.

1 *Ser.* Help, help, my Lord is fallen! my Lord is dead!
2 *Ser.* Oh! Heaven! What's the matter with my Lord?
3 *Ser.* He opens now his eyes!
4 *Ser.* He foams at the mouth.
1 *Ser.* Let's set him in the Chair and give him air.
3 *Ser.* I'le run for his Physitians.   *Ex.*
4 *Ser.* I'le give notice
To all the Court.   *Ex.*

Enter the three Murtherers.

Card. Stand off, and let the Duke of *Glocester* speak to me.
Speak, speak, I say! What wou'dst thou have with me?
  2 *Mur.* He names the Duke of *Glocester.*
  1 *Mur.* Oh! Does he so?
Is his Infallibility come to that? A Pox of his Doctrines,
He has damn'd himself and me too.
  Card. Who is the Grave-maker?
He is a Villain, he digs Graves so shallow,
The dead break Prison, and come plague the Living.
Why this is fine, the Living cannot eat
Nor drink, nor sleep in quiet for the Dead;
The Dead that can do none of e'm, must plague us.
Thou envious Ghost, get to thy own abode,
I know not where it is, in Heaven or Hell,
Oh! Hell! Hell! Hell! I am tormented: Oh!
  1 *Mur.* Oh! gallant, brave Infallibility!

Enter the King, Salisbury, Warwick.

King. How does the Cardinal?
  2 *Mur.* Sir, of a sudden
He's fallen into a fit of Infallible Madness.
  Card. Ha! who are these? Stand off, stand off, who are you?
  Sal. This is your King.
  Card. What King? The King of Terrors?
Death! is it he? If thou be'st Death, I'le give thee
Treasure enough to purchase all this Kingdom,
So thou wilt let me live, and feel no pain.
  King. Ah! What a sign it is of evil life
When Death's approach appears so terrible?
  War. My Lord, my Lord! Do you know your King?

Car.

Car. What King? what King?
War. King *Henry.*
Car. Ha! King *Henry!*
Sir, bring me to my Trial when you will,
I am prepar'd, died he not in his Bed?
Can I make men live whether they will no?
Oh! do not torture me! I will confeſs! ——Oh!
  King. Poor wretch!
  War. What think you, Sir? Are not theſe ſigns
Of horrid Guilt?
  King. Let us not Cenſure him.
  Car. Alive again, do you ſay? Ha! ſhew him me!
I'le give a Thouſand Pound to look on him.
Stand by and let me ſee him,—— there he is,
He has no Eyes, the duſt has blinded e'm,
Comb down his hair!——look!——look! it ſtands upright
Like Limetwigs, ſet to catch my flying Soul.
I prethee do not carry me along with thee,
And I'le do cruel Pennance all my life;
Hunger ſhall tear my Entrals, Whips my Fleſh,
Thorns my bare Feet; my habit ſhall be Hair-cloth,
The Rock my Bed, hard Roots my only food,
Foul Puddle all my drink; if this ſuffice not,
I'le ſell my ſelf a Slave among the *Turks*:
What doſt thou ſay? wilt thou conſent to this?
  King. Oh! thou eternal Mercy, caſt an eye
Of pity on this Wretch! Oh! drive away from him
The hungry Fiend, that ſtrives to gripe his Soul.
  Card. Ha! Wilt thou not conſent? and muſt I die?
Oh! let me live, and be a Slave, a Dog!
What muſt I die? Oh! this is very cruel!
  War. See how he grins, Sir, with the pangs of Death.
  Sal. Diſturb him not, let him paſs peaceably.
  King. Peace to his Soul, if it be Heavens good pleaſure,
Lord Cardinal, If you have any hopes of Heaven,
Hold up your hand, and give a joyful ſignal.
  Sal. He gives us none.
  King. Oh! Heaven have mercy on him.
  War. He gives a dreadful ſignal of his Guilt.
  King. Forbear to judge him, we are ſinners all.
He's dead!——cloſe up his eyes,——and let us all
To ſad and devout Meditation.

Exeunt.

The MURDER of the D. of GLOCESTER.

*The Scene is drawn. The Queen weeping.———
A Lady attending.*

Qu. How am I robb'd of all my joys in Youth?
That now my doleful Years will hang on me,
Like a great Family on a poor Bankrupt.
My hope is, Destiny will ne're be able,
With this great weight of Misery upon me,
To drag me to the Prison of old Age,
Where we lie cold and dark as in the Grave,
And have as great a load of Earth upon us;
Where melancholy thoughts about us crawl,
Like Toads in Dungeons about Malefactors:
That Prison, where through gates of Horror wrinkled
Fate feeds us with the Water of our Tears;
But enough to quench the thirst of Sorrow,
For the old Well is then almost dried up.
  Lady. Oh! Madam! you'l bring Age on you in Youth,
If you weep thus.
  Qu. I wou'd if I cou'd, bring on me
The only joy of Age to be near Death.
But I have a long Life to travel through,
Barren and comfortless as any Desert,
And I am spoil'd of all just at the entrance.

Enter another Lady.

  2 *Lady.* Madam, there's a Gentleman without
Come from aboard a Vessel, where the Duke
Of *Suffolk* lately was.———
  Qu. Oh! bring him!

Enter a Gentleman.

Oh! saw you lately, Sir, the Duke of *Suffolk*?
  Gent. Yes, Madam.
  Qu. Oh! How does he?
  Gent. Well, I doubt not;
He is at the end of an unhappy Journey.———
  Qu. In *France* already?
  Gent. In a better Country.———
Madam, forgive my zeal to my dear Lord.
I had the honour to be once his Servant;
And knowing well your Majesty did bear
A very great respect to his great Merit.

K   Came

Came to entreat you to revenge his Blood!
Qu. His Blood!
Gent. His Blood: See Madam, this was once,
The beauteous manly Visage of my Lord.
Shews the Duke of Suffolk's *Head.*

1 *Lady.* She faints! she dies! Oh! help for Heaven's sake.
2 *Lady.* She stirs; she's coming to her self again.
Qu. Why have you wak'd me from this pleasing slumber,
In which I had forgotten my vast misery?
Where is the bloody Spectacle you shewed me?
1 *Lady.* Away with it!
Qu. Shew it me again, I say.
Oh! barbarous and bloody Spectacle!
Is this the Noble Duke? Is this the man
That was the pride of Nature, *England*'s Ornament,
But now is *England*'s everlasting shame.
Oh! my dear murder'd Duke! Is this the meeting
Which we at parting promised to each other?
Love promis'd more than Destiny cou'd pay.
Who did this cursed deed?
Gent. A cursed Pyrate,
Who in the Rivers Mouth clapt him aboard,
And took the Duke and all of us his Prisoners.
The Duke they knew not till they spy'd his George,
And then he own'd himself, and for his Ransome,
Offer'd what sums of Gold they wou'd demand;
He chanc'd to be one *Walter Whitmore*'s Prize,
Who lost in Fight his eye.
Qu. And to revenge it,
He wou'd put out the Sun.
Gent. Yes, kill the Duke.
And he was stirr'd to greater insolence,
By that damn'd Villain, which they call'd their Captain,
Who said the Duke had murder'd good Duke *Humphry*,
Begger'd the King, lost *France*, and ruined *England*.
Nay, his foul Tongue did not refuse to spit
Dishonour on your Sacred Majesty,
And said the Duke had injur'd the King's Bed.
Qu. Impudent Villain!
Gent. For all which foul Crimes,
He said he wou'd revenge the King and Kingdom.
Qu. Bold bloody Villain.
Gent. The brave Duke on this,
Calling to mind his Birth was Calculated,
And it was told him he shou'd die by Water,

He

The MURDER of the D. of GLOCESTER. 67

He thought at first the Fiend had quibbled with him,
And he shou'd die by one who was call'd *Water*;
But then remembring that he was at Sea,
He found the Devil had two strings to his Bow,
So Saw himself encompast round with Destiny.
Then lifting up his Eyes to Heaven he smil'd,
As if he in his noble thoughts derided
The sport Fate makes with great mens Lives and Fortunes.
Then looking down with scorn on his base Enemies,
He gave a sigh, at which he nam'd Queen *Margaret*,
And with that grace he acted every thing,
He bowed his Head, and had it stricken off.

   Qu. Oh! execrable Villains! cou'd this face
Which govern'd me, not strike an awe in you?
Who were not worthy once to look up it?
And thou unfortunate gallant man!
Thy Wit, thy Valour, and thy delicate Form,
Were mighty faults, which the World cou'd not bear.
No wonder the vile envy of the base
Pursued thee, when the Noble cou'd not bear thee,
They cursed thee as the *Negroes* do the Sun,
Because thy shining Glories blackned e'm.
For which, Oh *England*! thus I pray for thee!
May'st thou ne're breed brave Man, or if thou dost,
Oh! let him be thy Ruine, or thou his.
May all thy Witty men be sadly Vitious,
Let sloth devour their Fortunes, Fools their Fame,
Lewdness their Souls, their Bodies Foul Disease.
May thy Wise Men be Factious, and head Fools,
If they be honest let e'm loose their Heads.
Let thy Brave Men against thy self be bravest,
Be Men at foreign, Devils at Civil War.
Let all thy Pious Sons with zeal run mad,
And make Religion thy Reproach and Curse.
May'st thou have all Religions to confound thee,
And none to save thee. —— Here a bloody Altar,
Oh! cruel *England*! hast thou made for me,
Therefore these bloody Prayers I make for thee.

   2 *Lady.* The King is coming, Madam.

Enter

Enter the King.

King. Oh! my Lord,
I bring thee frightful News, the Kentishmen
Are up in Arms, headed by one *Jack Cade*,
A Fellow who proclaims himself Lord *Mortimer*,
Descended from the Duke of *Clarence* Line.
He is marching towards *London*, in the head
Of a rude rugged merciless crowd of Peasants;
And all the way he proclaims me Usurper,
And vows to Crown himself at *Westminster*.
And in this great distress, to comfort me,
The tray'trous Duke of *York*, with a great Power,
Is marching hither too, and he proclaims
He comes but to remove the Duke of *Sommerset*,
But most believe he secretly intends
To reap the benefit of *Cade*'s Rebellion.
That I am like a Ship beset with danger,
Threatned with Wracking by the Kentish Storm,
Or to be Boarded by that Pyrate, *York*.

Qu. So! so my Curse on *England* springs already. (*Aside.*
Oh! this were Musick to me, were it not
Allay'd by the sad weeping of my Son,
Heir of these Noble Kingdoms; who, methinks,
Sighs in my Ear, Ah, Mother, for my sake
Pity the helpless King my unfortunate Father!
He was Crown'd King when he was nine Months old;
But if you do not aid him, his Misfortune
Will never suffer me to be a King.
For thy sake Princely Boy, I will assist him,
And something for his own, he's a good Man,
Though a weak King; and it was my ambition
Made *Suffolk* stain his hands in innocent Blood.
Which Crime forgive me Heaven, and let the Duke
Of *Suffolk*'s Blood be all my Punishment.

Enter Sommerset *and* Buckingham.

Buck. Oh! fly Sir, fly, the Rebels are in *Southwark*;
The Citizens through fear forsake their Houses.
The Rascal People all joyn with the Traytors,
Threatning to spoil the City, and your Court.

Som. Take comfort, Royal Sir, we'll all stand by you.

King.

The MURDER of the D. of GLOCESTER.

King. Pray let as little Blood be shed as possible.
I'le send a holy Bishop to entreat e'm
To spare their Souls and Bodies; I will promise e'm
To mend my Government, for I confess,
England may yet Curse my unfortuate Reign.
  Qu. Come, Sir, take Spirit in you; Men like Buildings
Fall to the Ground, if never Fire burn in e'm
To harden e'm; King's a Royal Building,
That shou'd have no soft Clay in it at all.
Adversity has always reign'd upon you,
And made you soft; but yield not, Sir, to Rebels.
Royalty like great Beauty, must be chaste,
Rogues will have all, if once they get a taste. *Exeunt.*

Epilogue.

Epilogue.

NOw some fine things perhaps you think to hear,
But he who did reform this Play does swear
He'll not bestow rich Trappings on a Horse,
That will want Breath to run a Three-days Course;
And be turn'd off by Gallants of the Town,
For Citizens and their Wives to Hackney on.
Not that a Barb that's come of Shackspears breed,
Can e're want Mettle, Courage, Shape, or Speed;
But you have Poetry so long rides Post,
That your delight in Riding now is lost.
And there is Reason for it I must own,
I'ave Foundred all the Poets in the Town.
Alas, their Strength and Courage may abate,
Under the Critique's Spur, and the Fools Weight.
And Destiny is playing wanton Tricks,
Turning the Nation round to Politiques;
The Romish Beast has scar'd her from her Wits,
And thrown her in her old Convulsion Fits.
The same she had many Years since, 'tis said,
Then Poetry was a miserable Jade.
The Pulpit then Men fiercely did bestride,
And Musqueteers that Wooden Horse did ride.
Those damn'd Diseases by time purg'd away,
The Nation streight grew Young again and Gay.
Balls assign'd, as Masquerades and Plays,
Were all the Business of those happy Days.
You flock'd to Plays as if they Jubilees were,
Things to be seen but once in Fifty Year.
Boxes i'th' Morning did with Beauty shine,
And Citizens then in the Pit did Dine.
The Wife with her good Husband did prevail,
To bring the Sucking Bottle full of Ale.
Then on her Knees cold Capon-legs were seen,
Her Husbands Capon-legs I do not mean.
Then we were pretious things, purchas'd tis known,
By Cloaths and Suppers, but these Days are done.
Yet they will come again, Times cannot hold,
But whilst they mend, Curse on it we grow old;
Then we may all who once were your delight,
Sup with Duke Humphry as you have done to Night.

FINIS.